After the Bell

After the Bell

Contemporary American Prose about School

EDITED BY
Maggie Anderson
& David Hassler

UNIVERSITY OF IOWA PRESS
IOWA CITY

University of Iowa Press, Iowa City 52242

www.uiowapress.org

Printed in the United States of America
Design by Sara T. Sauers

The University of Iowa Press is a member of Green Press Initiative and is committed to preserving natural resources.
Printed on acid-free paper

Library of Congress Cataloging-in-Publication Data
After the bell: contemporary American prose about school / edited by Maggie Anderson and David Hassler.
p. cm.
ISBN 1-58729-603-9, 978-1-58729-603-1 (cloth)
1. Schools—Literary collections. 2. School prose, American. 3. Education in literature.
I. Anderson, Maggie. II. Hassler, David, 1964– .
PS509.E36A36 2007
810.803557—dc22
2007007337

07 08 09 10 11 P 5 4 3 2 1

To our mothers, our first teachers,

Frances DeLancy Anderson 1908–1958
Diana Cain Hassler 1938–1976

Contents

Introduction xi

SHERMAN ALEXIE from "Indian Education" 1

MAGGIE ANDERSON In the Art Room 4

RANE ARROYO The Invisible Boy in a Jock 6

ESTHER ROYER AYERS from "Feeling Different" 9

PHYLLIS BARBER from *How I Got Cultured: A Nevada Memoir* 11

JAN BEATTY Flurry 15

MARK BRAZAITIS The Invisibles 16

CHRISTOPHER BUCKLEY My Time on Earth 19

DAVID CITINO Let's Move Our Chairs and Desks Around and See What We Can See 21

ROBERT COLES Here and Now We Are Walking Together 22

KATIE DALEY The Word according to Mr. Coosak 25

TOI DERRICOTTE from *The Black Notebooks: An Interior Journey* 28

ANNIE DILLARD from *An American Childhood* 31

MARK DOTY from *Firebird: A Memoir* 35

VIOLET A. DUTCHER Learning Politics in the First Grade 38

JOYCE DYER The Day I Stopped Hating Cheerleaders 40

LINDA DYER Votive 44

KATHY EVANS After the Facts: Poetry and the Sophomores 45

HENRY LOUIS GATES, JR. from *Colored People: A Memoir* 46

DIANE GILLIAM Does Not Use Free Time Wisely 48

RICHARD HAGUE from *Milltown Natural: Essays and Stories from a Life* 50

DAVID HASSLER Wrestling Mr. Dietz 52

RUTH ELLA HENDRICKS Professional Knowledge and Practice 54
WILLIAM HEYEN The End 55
FAITH S. HOLSAERT History Dancing 56
HANK HUDEPOHL Friday Night Heroes 60
LAWSON FUSAO INADA Our Song 64
JULIA SPICHER KASDORF Portrait of a Poet as a Public School Kid 66
GARRISON KEILLOR from "School" 70
JANE KENYON Dreams of Math 74
JESSE LEE KERCHEVAL from "Everything You Always Wanted to Know" 77
BARBARA KINGSOLVER How Mr. Dewey Decimal Saved My Life 80
LEONARD KRESS Yearbook 83
STEPHEN KUUSISTO from *Planet of the Blind* 84
PHILIP LEVINE from *The Bread of Time: Toward an Autobiography* 86
AUDRE LORDE from *Zami: A New Spelling of My Name* 88
PETER MARKUS I Am a Cloud: Revisited, or an Open Letter to My Third Grade Teacher 93
REBECCA McCLANAHAN Orbit 95
KENNETH A. McCLANE The Mitchell Movement 96
BRENDA MILLER from "Three Lessons" 101
NAOMI SHIHAB NYE Last Day of School 103
GREGORY ORR from *The Blessing* 107
VIVIAN GUSSIN PALEY from *Kwanzaa and Me: A Teacher's Story* 109
MAJ RAGAIN Under the Guidance of Falling Petals 113
ALBERTO RÍOS from "The Body of My Work" 118
SUZANNE RIVECCA The Music Teachers of St. Augustine's Elementary 122

LUIS J. RODRIGUEZ from *Always Running: La Vida Loca, Gang Days in L.A.* 125

RICHARD RODRIGUEZ from "Asians" 127

DAVID ROMTVEDT from "Some Shelter" 128

VERN RUTSALA Some of Us 130

SCOTT RUSSELL SANDERS The Real Questions 131

SUSAN RICHARDS SHREVE from *Tales Out of School: Contemporary Writers on Their Student Years* 133

THEODORE R. SIZER from *The Red Pencil: Convictions from Experience in Education* 135

LARRY SMITH from "My Working-Class Education" 139

GARY SOTO Catholics 141

MICHAEL STEINBERG High School Baseball Tryouts 143

JUDITH GOLD STITZEL Milk Money 146

LAWRENCE SUTIN One of the Men in the White Coats 148

ANNIE THOMS from *With Their Eyes: September 11th—The View from a High School at Ground Zero* 150

JANE TOMPKINS Reverie 155

BRUCE WEIGL Before and After 157

MEREDITH SUE WILLIS What I Learned in First Grade 159

Notes on Contributors 163

Acknowledgments 179

Introduction

As in our previous anthology, *Learning by Heart: Contemporary American Poetry about School*, the works collected here focus on the elementary and secondary school experience. While the poems in *Learning by Heart* offer condensed, musical, and sharply imagistic moments from life at school, the prose pieces in *After the Bell: Contemporary American Prose about School* allow more room for expanded narrative, detailed description, and reflection.

Out of our own interest in the relatively new genre of the short personal essay, we looked for pieces that were no more than 2,000 words in length. We looked for lyric intensity fueled by images, but we also sought an engagement with facts and issues and a good story that resonates beyond the merely anecdotal. After reviewing approximately 400 pieces in journals, books of essays, memoirs, and from among the over 150 submissions we received, we have included here 62 short essays by both new and well-established authors of poetry, fiction, essays, and educational theory and practice, nearly all of them teachers.

The works included take place in both public and private schools, in the classroom, on the playground, and on sports fields. They are composed from the point of view of students, teachers, parents, and administrators. Singly, they often present one moment of one day with one teacher that changed someone's life—for good or for ill. Collectively, they create a collage of the successes and failures of elementary and secondary education in the United States from the 1930s to the present. They tell a story of how we learn and how we teach, of what we carry with us from the first bell that begins the school day to the bell at the close of each day to the bell at the close of the year. As Naomi Shihab Nye notes, "There will never, never, be a last day of school."

School is the transom over which we must climb from the intimacy and secrecy of home to the mandatory public community. What we learn in that process is documented in these personal essays with the meticulous detail of children, who notice everything about their teachers and classmates—their hair, their clothes, their bodies, their habits. As David Citino observes about the moment of change in his essay "Let's Move Our Chairs and Desks Around and See What We Can See": "One thing school teaches is that everybody chews differently."

In the passage from home to school we are sometimes gently guided and warmly embraced by men and women who love learning and who genuinely love children. Our own teachers, the art teacher Miss Alber and the wrestling coach Mr. Dietz, were the embodiment of the great good teachers of American legend—the ones who taught both skills and the complexity of human emotions. Our own school-age years were shadowed by the early deaths of our mothers, and these teachers helped us articulate our grief through the languages of sport and art. In this collection also are the home-school teacher who sympathized with yet challenged the young boy enduring the effects of polio (Maj Ragain), the poet-in-the-schools who taught for only a few days but instilled in the young Julia Spicher Kasdorf the desire to become a poet, the high school librarian who "snatched" Barbara Kingsolver "from the jaws of ruin," and the wonderful Charity and Mimi, teachers in the progressive Little Red School House, who taught Negro and Jewish history, singing and dancing the Bunny Hop for the lucky children of Greenwich Village in the 1950s (Faith S. Holsaert).

Not every child is so fortunate. Others are abruptly pushed from the safety of home and greeted by the school and its teachers with suspicion and derision. It is bracing to discover how many adult memories of school focus on unkind, misguided, vindictive, loud, or even violent teachers. The sadistic Mr. Mitchell and Mr. Rodgers in Kenneth A. McClane's "The Mitchell Movement" torment young Kenneth out of their racism and their own bile and make him "understand in numerous ways that I was inadequate—in schoolwork, my desire to be creative, even in my desire to be *black*." And this at the Collegiate School in New York City, the oldest and one of the most exclusive private schools in the United States.

Sherman Alexie's memories of his reservation schooling, Henry Louis Gates, Jr.'s account of the accepted racism in his small West

Virginia town ("those rules that you didn't know existed until you broke them"), and Alberto Ríos's poignant account of trying, as a second-grader, to protect his parents from the teachers who forbade Spanish to be spoken in school demonstrate the ways in which school presents us with our first hard lessons of race and class. In school we are all taught several languages; we slowly, painfully become, if not literally bilingual like Ríos, then certainly multilingual, as we study the languages of class and occasion. We learn home talk and school talk, bus talk and classroom talk, gym talk ("gym class was about one's last name," Rane Arroyo writes), and public speaking. School is our first strict lesson in how we fit in (or don't), how we stand apart, and how we stand out.

These pieces are also rich in descriptions of the physical details of many different kinds of schools: the brick schoolhouse of Garrison Keillor's New Albion Academy; Kathy Evans's "portables," where she and the sophomores she teaches become "a new form of trailer trash"; Stuyvesant High School, four blocks north of the World Trade Center on September 11, 2001; Mark Doty's drama department, "a separate world from the rest of Rincon High School, squirreled away in a basement corner, darker and cozier than anything else in those acres of linoleum and fluorescent lights"; and Jane Kenyon's one-room country school, a "small, white clapboard building, complete with large bell, hunkered with its flagpole and swing sets in the midst of small farms and apple orchards."

While many of these writers recall a time long vanished, some facts about school remain immutable. In this country, still, school is mandatory. It is the one experience we all share as Americans. We live for ten to twelve years of our lives in a random and forced community that some will remember as a "correctional institution" (Lawson Fusao Inada) or that place where we "learn to sit still and listen" (Jane Tompkins). Others, like Gregory Orr, will find in school a place infinitely safer and freer than home: "There was nothing about school I didn't love. But most of all I cherished how simple, predictable, and responsive it was. In school, everything made sense and there were no mysteries, no shadows and silences." Still others are immediately confronted with hundreds of new and inscrutable rules and definitions that teach us to multiply our knowledge and divide ourselves (Violet A. Dutcher). All schooling is finally about the compromises we learn to make in order to navigate the most formative years of our lives, about how much—and how little—choice we have in that.

The essays in *After the Bell* are about the memories we have carried from our school days that both haunt and sustain us. They allow us to enter again the many worlds of school, the stuff of first grade as Alberto Ríos names it: "desks, pencils, cubbyholes, clay, chalkboards, paints, butcher paper, maps," and the stuff of high school: Friday night football, study halls, drama clubs, and yearbooks. As Jane Kenyon writes: "I still dream that I'm lost in the hallways of a school, looking for a locker which, once found, I cannot open because I have forgotten the combination." We invite you to read the names—Miss Avery, Miss Sharp, Mr. Coosak, Coach Kerchman, Miss Shreve—and to remember your own teachers' voices, your unresolved stories, and your ineradicable dreams.

After the Bell

SHERMAN ALEXIE

from "Indian Education"

FIRST GRADE

My hair was too short and my U.S. Government glasses were horn-rimmed, ugly, and all that first winter in school, the other Indian boys chased me from one corner of the playground to the other. They pushed me down, buried me in the snow until I couldn't breathe, thought I'd never breathe again.

They stole my glasses and threw them over my head, around my outstretched hands, just beyond my reach, until someone tripped me and sent me falling again, facedown in the snow.

I was always falling down; my Indian name was Junior Falls Down. Sometimes it was Bloody Nose or Steal-His-Lunch. Once, it was Cries-Like-a-White-Boy, even though none of us had seen a white boy cry.

Then it was Friday morning recess and Frenchy SiJohn threw snowballs at me while the rest of the Indian boys tortured some other *top-yogh-yaught* kid, another weakling. But Frenchy was confident enough to torment me all by himself, and most days I would have let him.

But the little warrior in me roared to life that day and knocked Frenchy to the ground, held his head against the snow, and punched him so hard that my knuckles and the snow made symmetrical bruises on his face. He almost looked like he was wearing war paint.

But he wasn't the warrior. I was. And I chanted *It's a good day to die, it's a good day to die,* all the way down to the principal's office.

SECOND GRADE

Betty Towle, missionary teacher, redheaded and so ugly that no one ever had a puppy crush on her, made me stay in for recess fourteen days straight.

"Tell me you're sorry," she said.

"Sorry for what?" I asked.

"Everything," she said and made me stand straight for fifteen minutes, eagle-armed with books in each hand. One was a math book; the other was English. But all I learned was that gravity can be painful.

For Halloween I drew a picture of her riding a broom with a scrawny cat on the back. She said that her God would never forgive me for that.

Once, she gave the class a spelling test but set me aside and gave me a test designed for junior high students. When I spelled all the words right, she crumpled the paper and made me eat it.

"You'll learn respect," she said.

She sent a letter home with me that told my parents to either cut my braids or keep me home from class. My parents came in the next day and dragged their braids across Betty Towle's desk.

"Indians, indians, indians." She said it without capitalization. She called me "indian, indian, indian."

And I said, *Yes, I am. I am Indian. Indian, I am.*

THIRD GRADE

My traditional Native American art career began and ended with my very first portrait: *Stick Indian Taking a Piss in My Backyard.*

As I circulated the original print around the classroom, Mrs. Schluter intercepted and confiscated my art.

Censorship, I might cry now. *Freedom of expression,* I would write in editorials to the tribal newspaper.

In third grade, though, I stood alone in the corner, faced the wall, and waited for the punishment to end.

I'm still waiting.

FIFTH GRADE

I picked up a basketball for the first time and made my first shot. No. I missed my first shot, missed the basket completely, and the ball landed in the dirt and sawdust, sat there just like I had sat there only minutes before.

But it felt good, that ball in my hands, all those possibilities and angles. It was mathematics, geometry. It was beautiful.

At that same moment, my cousin Steven Ford sniffed rubber cement from a paper bag and leaned back on the merry-go-round. His ears rang, his mouth was dry, and everyone seemed so far away.

But it felt good, that buzz in his head, all those colors and noises. It was chemistry, biology. It was beautiful.

Oh, do you remember those sweet, almost innocent choices that the Indian boys were forced to make?

SEVENTH GRADE

I leaned through the basement window of the HUD house and kissed the white girl who would later be raped by her foster-parent father, who was also white. They both lived on the reservation, though, and when the headlines and stories filled the papers later, not one word was made of their color.

Just Indians being Indians, someone must have said somewhere and they were wrong.

But on the day I leaned through the basement window of the HUD house and kissed the white girl, I felt the good-byes I was saying to my entire tribe. I held my lips tight against her lips, a dry, clumsy, and ultimately stupid kiss.

But I was saying good-bye to my tribe, to all the Indian girls and women I might have loved, to all the Indian men who might have called me cousin, even brother.

I kissed that white girl and when I opened my eyes, she was gone from the reservation, and when I opened my eyes, I was gone from the reservation, living in a farm town where a beautiful white girl asked my name.

"Junior Polatkin," I said, and she laughed.

After that, no one spoke to me for another five hundred years.

MAGGIE ANDERSON

In the Art Room

When I was eight years old, my mother was very ill and I had no words for my feelings. In fact, it took me another four years to comprehend fully that my mother was not coming back after she died. I don't remember anyone asking me how I felt, but I remember clearly the hours I spent in the art room of the Dwight School for Girls in Englewood, New Jersey.

I had always loved the art room. I loved the medicinal, spicy smells of the preserving sprays; the wet, cold smell of the pots of gray clay; the amiable mess that always littered the room with pencils, scissors, paper, open jars of paint, and dusty pottery shards. The art room was in the basement of the school, as were the dance and music rooms, and I have retained into adulthood a sense of basements as creative places where one might draw or paint or dance and sing, or simply wait for something surprising to appear out of the damp and mysterious dark.

I loved the way the light streamed through little windows above our heads, and I also loved the art teacher, Miss Alber. She was a tall, thin German woman with a heavy accent which caused her to use words awkwardly and sparingly, but which also gave the few things she said an added intensity and weight. She had perfectly straight black hair, so black it was almost blue, cobalt. It curved around her chin like a silhouetted valentine when she bent over me at the table. She spoke with her hands, gesticulating and drawing in the air or outlining a face or a piece of bark she wanted us to copy. I remember the feeling of her hands over mine as I molded the little dog that later cracked in the kiln because of my excessive detail with legs and ears. I can still feel her large, rough hands, grainy as burlap weave, pushing my small clumsy fingers against the wet clay.

During the time my mother was ill, I did poorly in school. Most significantly, I seemed to be losing the ability to read. Because I had been a good student—and a very good reader—my teachers decided this must be a temporary lapse related to the problems at home, the evening hours spent in hospital waiting rooms. They allowed me generous amounts of time away from the regular classrooms to go down into the basement art room with Miss Alber, the only place I seemed calm and focused. I was fascinated by the possibilities of color, and sometimes, while enthusiastically mixing paints, I would end up with a murky terrible green color, like a festering wound. Miss Alber worked with me to keep the colors pure, gently prodding, "If you keep adding so many things, you will make the sick color again. You must stop now."

In the spring of my mother's death, I had grown proficient enough with my color mixing that I had earned the honor of having two paintings hanging on the art room wall. Miss Alber was very discriminating in what she chose to display—only nine or ten pieces at a time—and for a few weeks, two of them were mine. I don't remember now what specific thing had happened the day I went into the art room and took my pictures down. I know I was determined, and calm, in the way people are calm just before they have to do something they know is dangerous but still must be done. I also knew it was wrong. I took my paintings to the far end of the room beside the pots of clay and the big iron sinks and laid them on the table and worked on them while Miss Alber worked on finger painting with a kindergarten class. By the end of class, I had colored both of my bright pictures totally black, using a fat black crayon and pressing very hard so they felt like slick oilcloth when I was finished. Immediately, I wished I had not done it. Although I expected to be punished, I brought the pictures to Miss Alber.

"Now you will make a new picture," she said. She led me back to the table with her hands on my shoulders. "This new picture will be different. Perhaps it will be even more beautiful than the others." She handed me a thin palette knife and showed me how to scrape the black crayon off the picture in some places so that a new image, full of color and odd abstract shapes, emerged from the palimpsest. I stayed in the art room with Miss Alber most of the rest of that morning, scraping hidden images out of the angry black, pushing the knife straight down into my grief, carving unexpected shapes in red and blue and yellow and green.

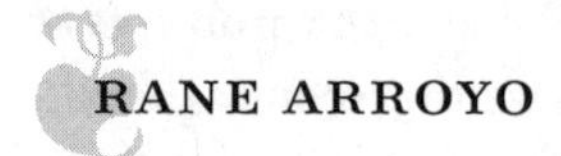

RANE ARROYO

The Invisible Boy in a Jock

I raised my hand, "What is a jock, Mr. Smith?"

Our earnest sixth-grade teacher was preparing us for junior high nightmares. The class laughed as Mr. Smith turned Isadora Duncan red. It was an honest question: what was a jock—and why the unscripted drama in the classroom?

We were an unfunded family. ("If it's not a book then we won't waste a penny on foolishness," Papi screamed at me in the Vatican City of his garage after I told him I needed some money for a field trip to see dinosaur bones.) I had to somehow justify the items on the stern shopping list that Mr. Smith had handed out, requirements that were accompanying us into puberty. My body was changing without warning. Every once in a while, it would pause so that my mind could catch up.

Mr. Smith stuttered, "You'll find out soon enough. Recess, everyone."

It didn't take much then to become a folk hero of the modern classroom. Boys who were the givers of black eyes sought me on the rusting monkey bars, "Cool. Men never blush. You did it!"

What had I done?

Still, I liked the sudden camaraderie of the bad boys. I howled with those future thugs. I howled with loud pride on the bland monkey bars. I was finally the accepted savage and no longer Rane-the-Invisible. The other boys seemed to hear me, see me.

One handsome boy sang, "This is for that fag who gave me a C in English."

What was a fag and why was English more complicated than the Spanish we spoke only at home? I liked being accepted, and shouted "jock" throughout that recess just to make the other boys laugh, several of them falling almost on cue on the concrete lawn of our childhood. We returned to the classroom and Mr. Smith avoided our eyes. We tortured Mr. Smith simply by smirking, most of us unsure of what new power we had somehow gained over him.

Mami saved "insane" (mad) money for my elusive jock (how much does a mystery cost?). I just said it was for gym, like gym shoes, like the shorts that could only be the color of tank gray, pigeon gray, or smoke gray. She had a system in which loose change magically transformed into a windfall. (Sometimes English was magical: "falling wind.") We went to the local drug store and began the Holy Grail search for the jock. Despite our family's code to keep to ourselves, I finally had to approach a pharmacist. He was white, old, and tall, and these were attributes that were always associated with "the enemy." No one had ever made clear to me why there was a war at all. It just was real.

"Sir, *Señor*, I need a jock," I said slowly to make sure he understood me.

He led us to a tall tower of boxes and pointed at them as if he was a mule that was about to be unloaded of ridiculous cargo. The pharmacist shrugged, "What size?"

Filled with panic, I answered, "Normal."

Later, in the illiteracy of home, I tried it on. It was just half of a fig leaf, a cold embrace. I refused to model it for Mami. She talked to me through the veil of the bathroom door, "Don't tell your father—he'll take it back and demand the rest of it."

Then junior high school began and it was time for the requisite gym class.

"Everyone better be wearing a jock or you'll fail this class and that means you'll fail life, get it?"

The gym teacher was an astonishing man, older (though now I realize he was probably no more than 23), and more like a triumphant movie star than the brain-dead drill sergeant others had warned me to expect. He made us all line up wearing just jocks to make sure we were being protected. From? We stood in front of our lockers, and I was proud not to be singled out like usual. Only two students were sent out of the locker room and their embarrassment was a Darwinian feast. It wasn't us who were being excluded!

"Get dressed boys," he said and we did, mocking the two pinkish boys drummed out of our first basketball game as we changed into the uniform of muscles and bragging.

I finished and turned to go when I saw my gym teacher step into his own jock. He looked up at me and smiled. "I'm not staying on the sideline!"

I nodded and he looked to me like a Greek statue, only somehow smuggled into the United States, into Illinois, into Carpentersville, into my consciousness, into a new country that would take me many years to know its name. His nakedness became more obvious in a jock. Something stirred in me that had nothing to do with him. The gym teacher was obviously unaware of how aware of him I was.

My body didn't look like his. When I had stepped into my jock a second time at home when no one was around, I felt harnessed, obvious, vulnerable, and oddly a braggart. Perhaps it was an excuse to look at myself, those years as the invisible boy finally ending.

He continued dressing. "I like that you dressed so fast. Shows you are focused. See you on the court. What's your name?"

"Arroyo," I replied, having learned that gym class was about one's last name.

"Arroyo, I'm your worst nightmare," he said, grinning.

ESTHER ROYER AYERS

from "Feeling Different"

I pledge allegiance to the flag of the United States of America, and to the republic for which it stands, one nation . . . I knew the words to this pledge, yet was not allowed to participate in the morning ritual.

"When your classmates stand and salute the flag, you must remain seated," my mother instructed when I first attended school.

And later, she added, "Old Order Mennonites are not allowed to salute the flag. We do not pay our allegiance to worldly governments. Our allegiance is to God and heaven."

Noting my discomfort with this rule, at times she added, "Esther May, it's very difficult being different, but you must remember that we are just pilgrims passing through this world. We keep our eyes focused on heaven. Our reward comes after we die. Someday we'll live in a place where there will be much joy and happiness. When you keep your eyes fixed upon this goal, it's easier to obey."

Indeed, Mama, I wanted to say. Do you know how difficult it is being different in a classroom when you're eight years old? You attended Germantown School in a one-room class filled with other Old Order children. If I asked, could you recite the pledge of allegiance? Did you even have a flag in your classroom?

But in an Old Order Mennonite family, children cannot ask such questions. It is of utmost importance that they obey their parents and the rules of the church.

Sarah and I shared the third-grade classroom because she had failed the previous year. It was better for me when I had no tattletale sister watching my every move. . . . Remaining seated during the flag ceremony didn't seem to bother Sarah. She concentrated on obeying Mama, which meant obeying the religion as well. Perhaps, being a year older, she felt she had rightfully acquired a certain matriarchal responsibility and took on the awesome position as guardian of my soul.

Having Sarah, so sweet and full of laughter, as custodian of my soul should have filled me with gratitude. Perhaps she urged me to be obedient so that we could continue our childhood games in heaven someday. Play house in heaven with our little teacups and saucers. She could serve me mud pies and I would pretend to eat them. Laughing. We would laugh together. What fun we would have!

And fun we did have when we played together. We'd share girlish giggles as higher and higher on the swing we'd go, our long skirts blowing in the air. What fun to play hide-and-seek, kick-the-can, and who's-got-the-button with her. Such joy I felt at home where we all dressed alike, behaved alike. But oh, those agonizing days at school!

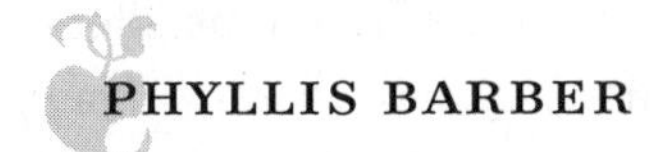

PHYLLIS BARBER

from How I Got Cultured
A Nevada Memoir

April. Sophomore year. Now or never. I knew I had to steel my way through this, not allow my body to rebel on me—my knees to shake, my nose to shine. With my babysitting money, I bought a glue-like deodorant to block all perspiration. I applied waterproof mascara and eyeliner to make my eyes large and cat-like with techniques I'd learned from my friend Ronnie Freed. I minimized my lips with a dark line drawn on by a new lipstick brush that clicked when the bristles came out and clicked when they went back inside. When the moon tried to talk to me and make me lose my concentration, I covered my ears with my hands.

And I kept my mother at bay. At the tryouts, I was like a Roto-tiller breaking up the soil, a disturbing machine determined to be noticed, determined to be a Las Vegas Rhythmette. Nothing else mattered.

In addition to the Saturday night dances, I'd stretched my legs into the splits all year to equip me with the highest kick, done one hundred sit-ups a night for a flat stomach, repeated exercises to increase my bra size. I chanted "I must, I must" while I pressed the heels of my hands together and pumped. And I watched for any idiosyncratic disruptions of solid rhythm. My heart was calcified.

On the day the new Rhythmettes were to be announced, I stood tightly packed in the middle of the twenty finalists who waited behind the locker-room door, listening to the castanets of "Lady of Spain" while the senior Rhythmettes did their last routine for the student body of Las Vegas High School. When the applause ended, the seniors lined up in a row at the opposite end of the gym. A thin black microphone stand had been set in place.

The finalists were hidden behind the locker room's slightly open door. Some were clinging to Saint Christopher medals, some were checking their hair in the mirrors, some were mumbling silent prayers. But everyone was secretly anticipating the sound of her name sailing across the empty gym floor, floating over the heads of all the students crammed into the bleachers, her name spoken into the microphone loudly enough for everyone in Las Vegas High School to hear, a name to be reckoned with and remembered.

The announcements started from the short end of the Rhythmette line. The shortest senior walked toward the microphone. She was handed an envelope. She opened it. She read it. She spoke the name. Cheryl Henry screamed and almost tore off the door's hinges getting out to the gymnasium where the green-painted bleachers were filled to capacity. Through the crack in the door that had been pulled closed again, I watched Cheryl run across the gym floor, her arms wide open until she slammed into the arms of the senior Rhythmette who'd called her name. They hugged and jumped like mayflies.

The next senior stepped out of her place in the line and up to the microphone.

I can't remember what happened then because the sound of the next name was so alien to the sound of mine. "Nancy Atkinson!" My ears went numb, arctic, and the whole room seemed a blizzard, with me huddling in animal skins, waiting for the cutter to break through the ice, throw a rope, and lift me. But I heard something through the storm's howling. Names being called. My name being called. Hands pushing me through the crowd.

"Phyllis, you made it."

I don't remember the trip across the gymnasium floor. I don't remember if people cheered or just clapped politely. After all, there were people out there who hadn't made the finals, people whose girlfriends hadn't made the finals, and here was I, Phyllis Nelson, a dark horse, walking, stumbling, running. I'd won. I'd controlled the elements, despite all the nattering from the moon.

I was slotted into place at the tall end of the line, and the music began. Squeezed between two other girls, shoulder to shoulder, I started across the floor. But a tiny moment of claustrophobia flashed through my head, so small I only remember it now. It had to do with eighteen dancing dolls and their choreography—always using the left foot to begin, turning their heads every eight counts, holding their shoulders back, tucking in their stomachs, smiling, always smiling as instructed by Miss Stuckey.

Crushed into my place in line and thinking in sets of four and measures of eight, I felt shut in for a brief second. What had I purchased? Another train ticket? For one small second I felt myself marching away from real rhythm where dancers threw themselves against the shadows of fire while the earth and the moon beat the drums. Real people howling at the moon, shaking their fists at the wind and the rain.

The new and the old Rhythmettes marched across the wooden floor. The line of girls was not the straight arrow line for which the Rhythmettes were famous, however. It rippled like water. We were Baby Rs, on our way to being grown-up and bounteous and leggy and ready for the grown-up world where our prancing legs would someday spread apart to make babies and birth babies or avoid babies or wonder why we couldn't have babies, all in accordance with the plan. We were being danced on our way by our hormones, by the mandate for procreation, by the rhythm of life, not knowing it was bigger than we were.

Dancing fools, me first among them, kicking headlong into our purpose on earth—to multiply and replenish. Miss Stuckey doing her part by preparing us with manners and stage presence, but really preparing us as gifts for the men who watched, men subject to their own hormones as we strutted and paraded across the stage, displaying our wares for them, the particular curve of our hips, the winning smiles.

The claustrophobia passed, however. I was one of the girls. A Las Vegas Rhythmette. I was somebody, and the football players and James Deans would have to reckon with me. . . . I counted now.

The bright colors of the moment caught my attention, and I exalted in the fact that I, Phyllis Nelson, had arrived. God bless America. And the stars and the moon. Even my seminary teacher. It didn't matter when I heard someone in the crowd filtering out of the gym saying, "How did Phyllis Nelson make it? She's so skinny. She walks like a primate."

And it didn't matter when my mother pretended to congratulate me. Her "Good for you, Phyllis," sounded hollow, echoing all the arguments we'd ever had about the importance of not getting sidetracked from God's work of being a lighted candle, virtuous, lovely, and of good report.

On that day in that time of my life, I could overlook all slights and forgive and bless everybody. I had arrived. I could dance up the stairway to the stars, clapping my hands and turning in sync with all other women who were ever girls. I didn't know my mother didn't need to worry. I wasn't privy to what the moon already knew. There's no escaping rhythm.

JAN BEATTY

Flurry

flurry. morning flurry of the young. boys in green ties. girls in gray plaid jumpers, running. to catholic school, then the scream, the dash, race to the glass door. the scream & the dash. race to the glass door of the foyer (green tile lobby of the suburban school). girls sprinting full out to beat the boys. no stopping before the red brick. (what stops us years later). learning. we can't beat them. really beat them. but this first year of many. wild mornings, all of us laughing in bunches. & crowding around him each day the same. flurry. young children, waiting to be swooped up. (waiting to be thought of). held too tight, youngness. held too long, kissed. the patting & hair stroking. I am his favorite. like your grandfather kisses you. he loves my oblivion. to his hands. he says he likes my smile. my 20 years before the charges are brought. my smallness. priest. stands in his black cassock. next to the list of movies. we are forbidden to see. by the holy statue. he swings us around. in his finery (next to the six-foot thermometer showing how hot). the chart of the money we raised. how close we are. to our goal. for the christian children's fund. it was him. there. in the lobby. our gray knee socks. our twirling young bodies. touching us.

MARK BRAZAITIS

The Invisibles

When I entered Woodrow Wilson Senior High School, one of D.C.'s largest public schools, I immediately felt small, insignificant, and adrift. The other two thousand students seemed cheerful and filled with purpose. I had, I was convinced, none of their good looks, none of their talent, and none of their confidence. The previous year I had completed ninth grade at the junior high next door, but I felt I was now in another country. And something else in my life was new and unwelcome: my nose, cheeks, and chin had been overtaken by acne.

After school, my classmates ran cross-country track or played soccer or rehearsed the Wilson Players' next show. When the bell rang at three every afternoon, I trudged home, ate a bowl or two of corn flakes, then slept. Sometimes I slept past dinnertime, which in the wake of my parents' divorce announcement that September tended to be a la carte. Sometimes I wouldn't wake up until my parents and sister had gone to bed. I liked being the only person awake in the house. No one could tell me what to do; my shortcomings were on display for no one.

Staying up until four in the morning made waking at eight difficult. Often I'd sleep in past homeroom period. My final sophomore year report card shows I was marked absent forty-one times.

I suspect I would have become more and more nocturnal, and would have arrived later and later to school, if I hadn't been encouraged—or ordered—to join the tenth-grade "It's Academic" team. My English teacher, a round woman with red freckles on her dark brown cheeks, handed me a flyer about the team's formation. "You should go to this," she said, speaking in the intimate, serious tone of someone suggesting a friend join AA.

The first practice was held in a third-floor science classroom with a waterless, algae-encrusted fish tank on the back window ledge. When I walked in, I knew immediately what crowd I had joined. I came to think of them, of us, as the "Invisibles." We hadn't joined the cross-country team; we weren't members of the chess club; we hadn't been elected to the student government. We were the people who vanished as soon as school ended. We were hardly noticeable during school hours.

As we waited for the faculty advisor to show up, we sat at our desks without speaking.

To say I fell in love with her when she first stepped into the classroom wouldn't be true but only because I didn't lift my head from my desk until she stood behind the large, slate-topped table in front of us and said, "Good afternoon."

She was obviously young; there were pimples on the sides of her face, although her acne seemed an intentional adornment, like small, ruby-colored tattoos. She had green eyes and dark blond hair, curly at the ends. She was a substitute Latin teacher, she explained. She probably wouldn't be around too long, but during her time at Wilson she was assuming all the responsibilities of the school's regular Latin teacher, who was on leave.

In a large army duffel bag, she'd brought the buzzers we were supposed to ring if we knew the answers to the questions she asked. She strung the buzzers over our desks like gray Christmas lights. Some of the buzzers proved to be dead, but this didn't seem to bother the players who were stuck with them. They could use the buzzers' malfunction as an excuse to preserve their torpor.

She shuffled the question cards before drawing one. "First question," she said, rotating her smile around the room. "What author wrote *Dead Souls*?"

It was like she'd given me a gift, spoken to my Russian-literature-loving heart. I slammed my buzzer. "Gogol!"

She seemed surprised that I knew the answer. More: she seemed impressed, delighted even. "Yes, very good. Very good."

In memory, I answered her first twenty questions correctly. But this couldn't have been true. The questions doubtless became harder, and while most of the other students were content to sit without so much as glancing at the buzzers in front of them, there were two boys on the other side of the room—fraternal twins who'd recently emigrated from Israel and dressed like students at a New England boarding school—who must have answered at least a few of her questions. But I am sure I answered more questions than anyone. And each time I answered, she gave me the same look, the same smile.

When our practice ended at four-thirty, she asked me if I would help her with the equipment. The other students didn't seem jealous that I'd been thus chosen; they left the room in a rush. "You have a quick mind," she said, and I carried these, her first private words to me, a long time, spoke them like a spell whenever I was alone and down.

I slung the duffel bag full of buzzers over my shoulder and hauled it down the three flights of stairs to her car. Her classroom, she explained, didn't have a locker or other secure storage space. "The administration prefers I keep them with me," she said.

"As if anyone would want to steal them to play at home," I said, which she found, to my amazement, funny.

The tenth-grade "It's Academic" team practiced on Mondays and Thursdays. The routine didn't vary much. We answered questions, sometimes competing as teams, sometimes as individuals. Our practices weren't aimed at helping us prepare for matches; only the school's official team competed against teams from other schools, in televised competitions. Theoretically, we were being groomed to assume spots on the official team the following year, but I knew of a tenth-grader who was practicing with the official team already. We were simply Invisibles prodded to become less invisible. Under different circumstances, I might have been cynical about it all and quit.

But I answered her questions—or as many of them as I could—as if each might be what I needed to foil the Sphinx and clear a path to her arms. And after every practice, I gathered the buzzers into the duffel bag and walked with her to her car. I don't remember most of what we discussed. I think I told her about my parents. I certainly told her about my love of Russian literature. She told me some things about her life—she liked French novelists, especially the existentialists; she spoke Italian fluently; she wanted to travel to India and ride on an elephant—but it's the tone of her voice I remember best. It was warm and said in texture, pitch, and color what it didn't say in words: *I know you. I understand.*

CHRISTOPHER BUCKLEY

My Time on Earth

I had changed schools mid-year in second grade, 1955, and had been at Our Lady of Mt. Carmel only a short while. Although I didn't know them all by name, I joined a group of boys and girls—Mexican, Filipino, and white—who took their lunches in back of the new pink and green stucco classroom. Brown sacks with baloney or tuna fish on white Webber's Bread, peanut butter and jelly on Roman Meal—all wrapped in wax paper—were opened without surprise. An apple or five-cent bag of Fritos, and after that we drank our pints of Golden State milk that the school handed out each noon—those cartons with leaf-green stripes all around, with the dairy's logo on one side like a cream-colored sun, a waxy cap in the corner you pulled up to open day after day.

In back of the new building there was a patch of wild grass, acacia and pepper trees, and a medium-sized boulder or two. We sat and ate quietly. We were only seven and easily overwhelmed with the larger world, and we were hungry. Someone climbed the low branches of a tree; one very skinny kid hung at arms' length from a bough. A couple of us leaned against the rocks; some just sat in the tall grass. There were maybe eight of us, working at halves of sandwiches our mothers had cut square in half or on the diagonal, crunching corn chips, content for the most part, just looking up. Above the deep green eugenia hedge that separated the school grounds from the property next door, we could see the mountains in back of Montecito, right at our backs really. Overhead, the white-as-soap-flakes fair-weather clouds cruised by, very low, it seemed to us. The sky domed over us, bluer than it would ever be again.

Only a day or two after joining my lunch group, I sat there and knew that I loved this, my beautiful life—the sky etched in the distance with palms, the daylight glistening among the trees and my friends, the still, bright seventy-degree air.

I would be there six more years, almost doubling my time on earth. I would grow up among the woods and creeks and know a sycamore from an oak from an acacia in no time at all. I would follow the creek trail to the beach and know the creatures in the surf and tide pools there. And though we would soon be moved from our Edenic spot to the new noisy lunch tables beside the rectory, though we would have to wait to be dismissed by the nun, table by table, to the playing fields, I knew that day that this was everything, that I was here for good.

The little Mexican girl I often sat next to was about as quiet as I was; I remember how the sky seemed to sparkle in her dark and happy eyes. And it was that first day I asked her, I guess, about our lunch break—"How long do we have?"

DAVID CITINO

Let's Move Our Chairs and Desks Around and See What We Can See

Each day of school is new, of course. Early morning, we and our parents, brothers, and sisters get dressed in different colors, shades, dots, and lines. The weather we come through to get to school is hotter or colder, more wet or dry. When we tromp into the school room, the chalk board is as fresh and green as an April field, as if wild flowers plump with bees and dew could sprout there as we watch and pay our best attention.

There's one day that's new above all others, though, that tickles up and down the spine, gives us a hot face, and moves and taps our feet. When teacher tells us she or he is changing our seats, we know the change will be the way we see our world and everything in it. We'll be close enough to smell the wonder of teacher's shampoo or we won't; we'll see our reflection in her or his glasses or we won't; and she or he will look at us first with every question, or only later, as eyes make their way down the rows filled with trees of raised arms and leafy hands all the way to the back wall.

The board will seem so close and sharp, or fuzzy and far. When teacher squeals the chalk, we'll shiver or we won't. The windows will get big or small, with more or less real daylight falling on our faces, the tops of our desks, and our paper as the hand holding the pencil makes its way left to right, line to line. Everyone we get to know best will become someone else, with brand new faces, whispers, and shoes on all four corners. Every fabric is its own smell, corduroy, denim, silk, and plain old cotton.

One thing school teaches is that everybody chews differently. Some mouths are soft and private. Some are loud, with smacks, satisfied sighs, and even gulps.

Changing seats and the way we see each day is scary but it's also quite exciting, quite nice. Before I leave this grade, I'd like to sit everywhere I could, meet and become close to every boy and girl in class—east, west, north, and south—and write what I think and feel in all different kinds of light.

ROBERT COLES

Here and Now We Are Walking Together

We all dreaded getting Miss Avery for the fifth grade—those of us in the fourth grade, awaiting the next year's classroom assignment. "She's tough," one of us remarked; "Real bad tough," affirmed another.

At the edge of change, we were mulling over our future. In so doing, we were dealing in our own way with larger matters that confront all of us human beings: luck, both good and bad, chance and circumstance, as they befall us, help shape our destiny.

So it went—American youngsters in the late 1930s, a terrible world war around the corner, a stern, demanding teacher who raised her voice and reportedly raised a stick, too (the blackboard pointer, which rumor had her using aggressively, punitively against those who earned her disfavor or worse). "You cross her, and she'll come at you," we'd heard.

I was assigned to "room five," where she supposedly reigned supreme, if not tyrannically. To this day, I see us all sitting in that classroom, headed by Bernicia Avery, a Vermont lady, heavyset, with white hair and alert blue eyes that darted everywhere and sometimes concentrated mightily, unrelievedly on the one of us who had gotten her ire up. To this day, also, I can hear the words that came my way one school morning: "Bobby! I've called your name twice before." Lifting my eyes, I realized how closely I was being watched by my fellow students, who knew well the dramatic possibilities immediately ahead: "This is a school," she bellowed. "You are not at home, alone in your bedroom or study room, reading a book on your own. You are here, with others, and we all deserve your attention as much as that book, valuable as it is!"

Our eyes met, stayed fixed on one another for a second or two—and then my head lowered. I stared at the book, then the floor beyond it. She had been sitting behind her big teacher's desk, but now she got herself up. Ominously, she had a ruler in her right hand—not the notorious blackboard pointer, thank God, but a

12-inch ruler. *Bang*. That ruler went crashing on the desk of Sally Davis, sitting on the first desk's seat, four or five ahead of mine (we tall boys got put farther back, a measure of "God's grace," to use an expression Miss Avery herself summoned every once in a while, when she wanted to explain the apparently inexplicable—a merciful turn of events that happened for no apparent reason).

As she began her walk, she spoke: "We are entitled to travel on our own paths, but here and now we are walking together." I finally lifted my eyes to acknowledge the speaker, the ruler of us seated young ones who had all attention focused on her magical (malevolent, some in the room thought) right arm, held a bit high. Suddenly she waved the ruler briefly and then *crash* on Doris Newman's desk, whose occupant memorably flinched, we all sure enough noticed.

Then, this terse finale, which six decades later holds fast to my head's awareness. "We should pay attention to others, as well as ourselves." A pause, while we took in the admonition. "We spend time looking at ourselves and looking out for ourselves, but please, let us look to our right and to our left, to our front and to what's going on to our back. Please, let us be mindful of others, as we hope they will be of us!"

Then, to our considerable surprise, she was at the blackboard, not in pursuit of that famously feared pointer but with chalk in her right hand. Word for word she scratched the message out for us, now to notice hard and long. When she was through with the chalk, she asked us all to read out loud, in unison, those words: a classroom's chorus to a written moral aria.

Needless to say, we obliged, even as we noticed our teacher giving her spoken best to the words she had dispatched in our direction. When we'd all finished, she suggested that we salute the American flag. Puzzled, surprised, at a loss, we nevertheless went along—a relief, maybe, to be going through ethical rote, rather than the reflection that had been prompted in us.

Back home that day's afternoon, I told my mother of the instruction offered us. We'd all been told to write down what our teacher had called for us to witness and consider—and there it was, now mine, in my hand, for my mom to contemplate. She read my words quietly, then read them out loud—not to me, but to herself. I can see her looking out the window, often her wont, then her eyes directed at me, and then her words: "If more people lived up to those words, the world would be a better place to live." Yes, I sure agreed in my thinking—my mother now had linked arms with my teacher, and I was very much a link between them.

Soon enough, we were on to other matters, tasks—my mom cooking and I readying myself, with some milk and cinnamon buns, for strenuous playing outdoors. As I left I noticed my mother still looking at my scribble—and then her decision to pin it on the bulletin board she kept for herself in the pantry. She saw me seeing and said: "We've got to look out for other people, as well as for ourselves." She'd repeated what we'd heard said in school, but her voice told her son, perched between home and the street, that this maternal declaration was deeply felt and so ought to be kept in mind for the future days to follow in such abundance.

Here I am, in another lifetime, so to speak, remembering Miss Avery and her times of tough insistence: a teacher who wanted us to learn our letters and numbers, yes, but a teacher who also wanted to keep us a bit free of the self-preoccupation that tempts us often, a bit free to turn outside ourselves so we might be fellow citizens to others. A big freedom, indeed—to be pushed now and then from the mind's inevitable self-consciousness in the direction of our fellow wayfarers and citizens, human inwardness given the outward life of human connection—an expressive and introspective freedom that both defines our humanity and gives it the sovereignty of enactment in the everydayness of our time spent here living with others as well as ourselves.

KATIE DALEY

The Word according to Mr. Coosak

In the fall of 1967, our history teacher at St. Christopher's parochial school was Mr. Coosak, a tall bachelor chain smoker with craggy good looks and an avant-garde interpretation of our Roman Catholic *History of the World* textbook. Despite the fact that he worked us hard and tolerated no excuses or horseplay, we felt a certain kinship with this semi-angry, semi-hipster, semi-sexy layman who strolled into our classroom every morning at eleven o'clock. And because he'd obviously ventured far beyond our little home town in the Smoky Mountains, we were eager to believe every word that shimmied out of his smoke-stained mouth.

According to our textbook, human history first set up shop with Adam and Eve, and the universe revolved around Rome. Every major event rippled out from the Pope or God. There was no China until Marco Polo discovered it, and the world was flat until the Vatican declared it round. But Mr. Coosak had much more intriguing tricks up his sleeve. Nearly every page of the way, he pointed out all the secrets the book was keeping from us. It was the most titillating instruction in critical thinking I've ever received.

One morning, after giving us the breakdown on Georgian royalty, he turned to us and said, "Now. About these ladies-in-waiting. Have you ever wondered what they were waiting for?"

Well, yeah, now that he mentioned it, I had. I wondered the same thing about most ladies, including my mother and the other women in our neighborhood, whose hair was as stiff as their girdles and who never whooped with glee or, for that matter, anything at all.

After scanning the room to make sure we had the requisite amount of curiosity about King George's ladies, Mr. Coosak erased his diagrams of royal bloodlines and wrote in huge letters that spanned the entire width of the chalkboard:

F.U.C.K.

Utter silence sashayed into the classroom, tossed its head at us, and draped itself like Cleopatra across Mr. Coosak's desk. Here and forever ceased all picking of noses, all passing of notes, all wadding of spitballs, all twanging of trainer bra straps. We stared back at The Word, wide-eyed and dumbfounded. We stole glances at Jesus on his crucifix above the blackboard, but he merely gazed down on our newest lesson as sadly as he ever had. After relishing our shock for several moments, Mr. Coosak folded his arms and said, "All right, wipe those stupid looks off your face. I know this word is not new to you. You've seen it on the walls of bathroom stalls. Some of you say it as much as you can when you're out of adult earshot. And if you don't know what it means by now, I'm about to tell you." Then he leaned down and filled in the letters between each initial until it spelled out the weird news: **F.**ornication **U.**nder the **C.**rowned **K.**ing.

I was stunned. All those haughty ladies in silk bustle gowns were waiting for the king to *F.U.C.K.* them? They had nerve endings and desire under those prissy clothes? They actually lined up to lift those petticoats and perform that shivery, greasy shadow act with the king?

Well.

Well, okay.

Well, but wait a minute. If ladies waited in line so openly to do it, and if the deed was named after kings' daily habits, why was it such a big deal secret now? Why hadn't it shown up in the fairy tales, or the war stories?

But after a few months under Mr. Coosak's tutelage, I already knew there were whole continents of information the adults were excommunicating and banishing into the black holes of the universe. The Big Bang. The eons of life that preceded Abraham. The various mistresses and misdeeds of popes. If I had a choice between versions of reality, Mr. Coosak's won hands down every time. Especially now that he'd dared to broadcast the most electric, gunpowdery password in our pubescent lives, dared to lift it from the chintzy lavatory walls and inscribe it so extravagantly across the entire front of our classroom. We gaped at the blackboard, which was bordered by stars for good behaviorites and the names of lunch time detainees, and saw the ghosts of our former selves gaping back at us: squirming rows of girls- and boys-in-waiting.

And what had we been waiting for? The forced confessions to be over? Someone in a black robe to dismiss us? For our real sins, our real lives, to begin?

Tonight, thirty-eight years after the most stupendous morning of my primary education, I googled "F.U.C.K." and "Ladies-in-Waiting." According to Jesse Sheidlower, who wrote *The F-Word* (Random House, 1999), "Fornication Under the Crowned King" is one of many urban legends developed in the 1960s about the origins of "fuck." Etymologists agree that the word probably crept into Middle English in the fifteenth century, influenced by several cognates in other Germanic languages: Middle Dutch *fokken*, meaning to thrust, to copulate with; dialectical Norwegian *fukka*, meaning to copulate; and dialectical Swedish *focka*, meaning to strike, push, or copulate.

Okay, so Mr. Coosak F.U.C.K.ed up. He didn't check his facts. Still, his version of history had much more human truth in it than that Roman Catholic textbook ever dreamed of revealing. And I continue to be deeply grateful to him for being the first adult to care enough to shake my world. He threw salt into my wound of ignorance and gave me the wondrous confirmation that the folks in charge were much more human than they let on to be, much more naked, much more consumed with desire, and much more crooked. They were as naughty as, and much, much naughtier than, we were.

This revelation was an enormous relief to me. It made my murky home life, complete with a father's infidelities and a mother's bitter silences, seem a little more common and considerably more bearable. And although I had little experience with physical desire, I recognized that this news of lustful ladies who cavorted with anyone, the king or otherwise, could be very promising. It rendered the prospect of becoming a woman decidedly more interesting and offered a fantastic potential for whooping.

It doesn't matter to me that the story itself wasn't exactly, literally true. It was a hell of a lot truer than anything else they were giving us. And the folks in charge now are laying it on just as thick as they ever have. Thanks to Mr. Coosak, the Big Bang, and the continuously sad gaze of Jesus, I've learned how to know better, how to keep alive the memory of a world that's much more curious, frisky, terrible, and hopeful than anything they could tell me.

TOI DERRICOTTE

from The Black Notebooks
An Interior Journey

LIGHTNING BUG

I asked the children to do a self-portrait with words. One girl, a black girl, Alicia, didn't like the way she looked. I told her that for everything she named that she didn't like about herself, I would name one thing I didn't like about myself.

She named teeth.

I named stomach.

She named fat.

I named feet.

She named hair. She named skin. This little girl in the second grade thinks she is ugly because of her hair and skin. She said the only pretty girl in class is Tracy—the white girl.

I sat down next to her and told her how, when I was in second grade, all the girls were drawing pictures of white women—movie stars—and saying when they grew up they wanted to look like them. I asked her if she understood what I was saying. She said I was trying to tell her that she would never be white.

I told her yes, in a way I was saying that.

Another girl in class said if you were going to a Black Muslim school, you would think white people were ugly.

I told Alicia that she *was* beautiful, her hair, her eyes, her skin, her nose. I told her the most beautiful thing about her is the energy inside her which is so full and bright it bursts out as if she has a lightning bug inside. She wrote this poem.

My name is Alicia.
Mrs. Derricotte thinks I'm pretty.
She says I have a lightning bug inside me.
And that makes me smile.

BABY PICTURES

I had asked the fourth graders to bring in baby pictures. I was going to play a game with them: have them guess which picture belonged to which fourth grader, talk about being a baby, and write. That morning, as the children mixed their pictures in a pile, the face of the only black girl in the room came at me with new clarity. I sensed this game might put her in danger.

The children fumbled over several pictures, guessing, "Tracy?" "Sharon?" When I held up Deborah's picture, they didn't hesitate. "That's Deborah," they said in unison.

Deborah looked shocked. "How did they guess me so fast?" She looked hurt, as if she had been discovered in a good hiding place. "How did they know it was me?"

Either the children didn't consciously know or else they were ashamed to say. One girl said, "You can tell by her brother standing next to her."

I thought of the way Deborah sits in the last seat, in the last row, as far back as possible, still she sticks out like a sore thumb. "That's Deborah," they had all said in unison.

Her face fell in disbelief. She came up to look at the picture, trying to discern what had given her away. She held it up, turning it, talking to herself, "But how did they know that was my brother?"

CLARISSA

My friend Mady said how disturbed she was about racial problems in the small town she's teaching in. The community is largely white and upper-middle-class. However, there is a poor black section. Many of the mothers in this section are maids in the households of other children in the school. In each class there is one black child, and this child is also outstanding in terms of behavior. In one class, the girl is super bright, super personality; in another the girl is the slowest. When asked to write something about her hand, she wrote: "My hand is clean." The teacher said, "That girl comes to school every day smelling and dirty." In other classrooms, the black children are either the clowns or the "bad" kids, almost all of them far behind. When Mady talked to teachers, they looked at her like she was crazy. "There's no racism here!"

I remember Clarissa, that girl who came to school each day starched and pressed all over—her kinky curls, her pinafore. I think of her oiled, gold skin, her knobby knees and thin calves like a filly's. She always talked at the wrong time, stood up at the wrong time, had to go to the bathroom. "Clarissa, didn't you go when the other children went?" And no matter how clean she was when her mother sent her, no matter how many times she brought home bad reports, each day Clarissa screamed as if crazy.

I think of the teacher lifting her, screaming, away from the dollhouse where the other girl whines, "She's taking my doll," holding her kicking feet away, carrying her down the hall at arm's length to the office, as if she had the plague. Clarissa screams for her body lifted against her will, screams because her mother will beat her, screams because she will sit all morning in the window of the principal's office where everyone will see.

How did this happen? By first grade it is already too late, and in spite of her mother, who spent her maid's paycheck on a white pinafore so that Clarissa would fit in, she *doesn't* fit in, and her mother isn't strong enough to beat that devil out of her.

What makes Clarissa jump out of her skin?

ANNIE DILLARD

from An American Childhood

Throughout the long, deadly school afternoons, we junior and senior girls took our places in study hall. We sat at desks in a roomful of desks, whether or not we had something to do, until four o'clock.

Now this May afternoon, a teacher propped open the study hall's back door. The door gave onto our hockey field and, behind it, Pittsburgh's Nabisco plant, whence, O Lordy, issued the smell of shortbread today; they were baking Lorna Doones. Around me sat forty or fifty girls in green cotton jumpers and spring-uniform white bucks. They rested their chins on the heels of both hands and leaned their cheeks on curled fingers; their propped heads faced the opened pages of *L'Étranger, Hamlet, Vanity Fair*. Some girls leaned back and filed their nails. Some twisted stiff pieces of their hair, to stay not so much awake as alive. Sometimes in health class, when we were younger, we had all been so bored we hooked our armpits over our chairs' backs so we cut off all circulation to one arm, in an effort to kill that arm for something to do, or cause a heart attack, whichever came first. We were, in fact, getting a dandy education. But sometimes we were restless. Weren't there some wars being fought somewhere that I, for one, could join?

I wrote a name on a notebook. I looked at the study-hall ceiling and tried to see that boy's familiar face—light and dark, bold-eyed, full of feeling—on the inside of my eyelids. Failing that, I searched for his image down the long speckled tunnel or corridor I saw with my eyes closed. As if visual memory were a Marx brothers comedy, I glimpsed swift fragments—a wry corner of his lip, a pointy knuckle, a cupped temple—which crossed the corridor so fast I recognized them only as soon as they vanished. I opened my eyes and wrote his name. His depth and complexity were apparently infinite. From the tip of his lively line of patter to the bottom of his heartbroken, hopeful soul was the longest route I knew, and the best.

The scent of shortbread maddened me in my seat, made me so helpless with longing my wrists gave out; I couldn't hold a pen. I looked around constantly to catch someone's eye, anyone's eye.

It was a provocative fact, which I seemed to have discovered, that we students outnumbered our teachers. Must we then huddle here like sheep? By what right, exactly, did these few women keep us sitting here in this clean, bare room to no purpose? Lately I had been trying to enflame my friends with the implications of our greater numbers. We could pull off a riot. We could bang on the desks and shout till they let us out. Then we could go home and wait for dinner. Or we could bear our teachers off on our shoulders, and—what? Throw them into the Lorna Doone batter? I got no takers.

I had finished my work long ago. "Works only on what interests her," the accusations ran—as if, I reflected, obedience outranked passion, as if sensible people didn't care what they stuck in their minds. Today as usual no one around me was ready for action. I took a fresh sheet of paper and copied on it random lines in French:

> *Ô saisons, ô châteaux*!
> Is it through these endless nights that you sleep in exile
> Ô million golden birds, ô future vigor?
> Oh, that my keel would split! Oh, that I would go down
> in the sea!

I had struck upon the French Symbolists, like a canyon of sharp crystals underground. These poets popped into my ken in an odd way: I found them in a book I had rented from a drugstore. Carnegie and school libraries filled me in. I read Enid Starkie's Rimbaud biography. I saved my allowance for months and bought two paperbound poetry books, the Penguin *Rimbaud* and a Symbolist anthology in which Paul Valéry declaimed, "*Azure! c'est moi . . .*" I admired Gérard de Nerval. This mad writer kept a lobster as a pet. He walked it on a leash along the sidewalks of Paris, saying, "It doesn't bark, and knows the secrets of the deep."

I loved Rimbaud, who ran away, loved his skinny, furious face with the wild hair and snaky, unseeing eyes pointing in two directions, and his poems' confusion and vagueness, their overwritten longing, their hatred, their sky-shot lyricism, and their oracular fragmentation, which I enhanced for myself by reading and retaining his stuff in crazed bits, mostly from *Le Bateau Ivre*, The Drunken Boat. (The drunken boat tells its own story, a downhill, downstream epic unusually full of words.)

Now in study hall I saw that I had drawn all over this page; I got out another piece of paper. Rimbaud was damned. He said so himself. Where could I meet someone like that? I wrote down another part:

> There is a cathedral that goes down and a lake that goes up.
> There is a troupe of strolling players in costume, glimpsed on the road through the edge of the trees.

I looked up from the new page I had already started to draw all over. Except for my boyfriend, the boys I knew best were out of town. They were older, prep-school and college boys whose boldness, wit, breadth of knowledge, and absence of scruples fascinated me. They cruised the deb party circuit all over Pennsylvania, holding ever-younger girls up to the light like chocolates, to determine how rich their centers might be. I smiled to recall one of these boys: he was so accustomed to the glitter of society, and so sardonic and graceful, that he carried with him at all times, in his jacket pocket, a canister of dance wax. Ordinary boys carried pocket knives for those occasions which occur unexpectedly, and this big, dark-haired boy carried dance wax for the same reason. When the impulse rose, he could simply sprinkle dance wax on any hall or dining-room floor, take a girl in his arms, and whirl her away. I had known these witty, handsome boys for years, and only recently understood that when they were alone, they read books. In public, they were lounge lizards; they drank; they played word games, filling in the blanks desultorily; they cracked wise. These boys would be back in town soon, and my boyfriend and I would join them.

Whose eye could I catch? Everyone in the room was bent over her desk. Ellin Hahn was usually ready to laugh, but now she was working on something. She would call me as soon as we got home. Every day on the phone, I unwittingly asked Ellin some blunt question about the social world around us, and at every question she sighed and said to me, "You still don't get it"—or often, as if addressing a jury of our incredulous peers, "She still doesn't get it!"

Looking at the study-hall ceiling, I dosed myself almost fatally with the oxygen-eating lines of Verlaine's "The long sobs / of the violins / of autumn / wound my heart / with a languor / monotone."

MARK DOTY

from Firebird
A Memoir

Drama class is my high school's haven for the odd and misbegotten, the dreamy and peculiar. Under the stage lights, in the workshop or at the makeup mirror, we turn out to be possessed of gifts no one could have foreseen; we turn out to be somebody after all, down in the Drama Department, which feels like a separate world from the rest of Rincon High School, squirreled away in a basement corner, darker and cozier than anything else in those acres of linoleum and fluorescent lights.

Mr. Frakes, the prince of our theatrical zone, is one of those rare teachers of young people who have no interest in holding power over anyone. He is courtly, self-possessed, consistently well-mannered in any circumstance. Dapper and donnish in rimless glasses and salt-and-pepper hair, he has such an obvious respect for intelligence and creativity that it startles me. I have never met anyone whose intellectual life is so democratic: He likes ideas themselves, not just his idea. He likes the arts, not merely his art.

His overriding passion is for the theater itself, and he assumes that anyone who's entered into the little city over which he presides (black box theater, dressing rooms, workshops, warehouse of old props) shares his passion, or wishes to. This assumption amounts to respect; what we do is collaborative work, our common shoulders turned to the play at hand, which is sometimes tired and crowd pleasing (*You Can't Take It with You* or *Dark of the Moon*) but more often something Mr. Frakes loves: Beckett, Anouilh, Shaw. We can't do Sam Shepard (too much profanity) but we do—unheard of in a high school—Jean-Claude van Itallie and Megan Terry, the new plays of the hour.

And so we find our way downstairs, to him and to one another, the kids who belong exactly there, the ones too thoughtful and idiosyncratic to find their place upstairs or, God forbid, in the gym. We're the kids who seem to carry our inner lives right in front of our faces, and in the Drama Department it is suddenly just right, just perfect that you live in your interiority. Here we prize strangeness; one of the new words that enters my vocabulary is "bizarre," offered as a compliment, in admiration, an all-purpose assertion of praise.

I've begun to shift my style. Out go the smoked plastic glasses, replaced with sharp new oval wire-rims. And I've taken to avoiding or refusing haircuts, and have arrived at a stylish length like the Beatles on the cover of *Sgt. Pepper's*, and suddenly I'm getting it: I have a new status in the eyes of my peers. I'm a person whose opinions and interests matter. It's the beginning of sophomore year, and I'm in Advanced Placement English, reading Fitzgerald and e. e. cummings. A new English teacher—bearded, hirsute, all that body hair somehow like an expression of his simmering nervous energy, as if he's literally *wired*—has us pull our desks into a circle and discuss Ferlinghetti poems (I dislike them even then), as well as give ourselves our own grades. We think he's ridiculous but entertaining, and he's fired in about three weeks. No matter, we go on with *The Great Gatsby* anyway; my new glasses, it occurs to me, must resemble the pair of spectacles on that spooky sign mounted out on Fitzgerald's Long Island dunes.

Something new's happening. I am relaxing into myself; tasting what it's like to approve of myself a bit because other people do; if you're a cool kid, then you're not a sissy, at least not till fourth period, after lunch, and the daily forced march to the locker room. We're creating a new category, in our school, my friends and I, a social niche to serve as an alternative to soshes (yellow windowpane plaids, canvas belts) and cowboys (stiff Wrangler jeans, white T-shirts) and hoods (greased or ratted hair, eyeliner, black leather). Or rather, we're absorbing something that's happening out there in the wider world, an emergent category of otherness. We're about to be what we'll call "freaks," and some of us couldn't be happier about it; the label denotes a stylish, desirable otherness. Heaven only knows how many of us, downstairs in the drama club, were young homosexual men and women; that aspect of ourselves simply did not come under examination, was not made visible in our new category. A freak, by definition, wasn't a sissy, wasn't queer. It was a form of liberation, strangely, this new place to dissemble, the best place yet to hide. One day I solidified my new fame by going to school in a shirt I'd made myself, a simple dashiki cut from an Indian block-printed cotton bedspread in a soft print of yellow and orange paisley shapes. Simple, you just cut out two pieces and stitch them up by hand with a needle and thread. Voilà: a new world, heady, its horizon nowhere in sight.

VIOLET A. DUTCHER

Learning Politics in the First Grade

Helping teacher after school feels good. She likes me. I can tell. Common as dirt after school she is. Inside, I help teacher sweep the wood floor with a lopsided broom, swirls of yellow chalk dust in the air. In the corner, I finally get to run my fingers through the cool sand. This is the boys' place, where they drive their Tonka tractors and trucks through trails mapped in this sand contained by a faded green wooden box. Outside, I help teacher beat the erasers on the red brick school wall.

I gather up my courage and tell Miss Mast a secret, something big girls do. Tell secrets that is. I tell her that awhile back, after school, Rachel and I talked Dutch while together in line behind the gray post, waiting for the bus. Talking Pennsylvania Dutch is *verboten*, forbidden to students on the playground, before and after school. We say morning good-byes to our mothers and baby brothers and sisters in Dutch. And then our lips are sealed until, in the afternoon, we step off the bus at the end of the lane. But that day, I got up my nerve to answer Rachel in Dutch, daring God to cut out my tongue on the spot. Just like that. So, I told Miss Mast. I laughed at Rachel and me as I told it. She smiled back, preoccupied. She likes me. And I like being here with her.

Next day right before recess I'm opening the silver latch on my red and blue plaid metal lunch box. Not again! Butter and homemade grape jelly smashed on soft white bread. The jelly bleeds through the bread, showing purple. I promise myself for the thousandth time never to eat food like this when I grow up. I look up from my little jelly jar of canned peaches to see Rachel's face turned back toward me from her desk in the front of the room. Her facial muscles are twisted down, and her eyes are fierce with disgust. Miss Mast has betrayed me. She has decreed to the whole class that Rachel and I must give up our recess today for talking Dutch while waiting for the bus. Rachel denies it. Says no such thing happened. I insist that it did. I don't lie. It's bad.

Inside me, I know something that day. I know not to tell secrets to Miss Mast. I know not to tell secrets to people who are the boss. I know Rachel is not my friend. I know to watch out for Mennonite girls. This is my own truth. Outside, I learn to be nice. To give in. To not make a fuss. To steer clear of conflict. In this way, I multiply my knowledge and divide myself. In first grade.

JOYCE DYER

The Day I Stopped Hating Cheerleaders

Until my junior year of high school, I hated cheerleaders. I sometimes imagined piling them all in a bus and driving it over a cliff, just before *I* rolled out to safety.

I hated cheerleaders because no matter how hard I tried, I never made the squad. And I did try hard.

I went to cheerleader camps in the summers. And during the school year, I watched those pretty girls all the time, trying to figure out what I'd have to do to be like them.

My cousin Sandra was a cheerleader. I wrote a paper about her for an eighth-grade assignment on biographies—"Write about the most famous person in your family." I didn't really like her, but she was a math whiz and her school's valedictorian, so I chose her. The real reason had nothing to do with her academic success, however, though my parents and her parents thought it did, and were happy my cousin apparently was having such a good influence on me. I chose her mainly because she was a four-year varsity cheerleader. I hoped that when I interviewed her for my paper she would let some of her secrets slip.

Like, how do you actually *do* a split?

I remember asking my high-school girlfriends to push down on my shoulders until my legs formed perfect right angles with my trunk, but there were always a couple of inches between my crotch and the carpet or lawn below me, even when they pressed hard. In *Life Magazine* I found a picture of a ballerina holding one of her legs straight up in the air and of the Radio City Rockettes doing high kicks. Where did these one-legged creatures come from? They seemed a different species from me.

I found out fast that my body was not designed for cartwheels, splits, or handstands. My legs were thin, my neck was long, and when I stepped on the gym floor at school dances, the most my graceless feet could do was break into the shuffle-ball-change I'd learned at Jean Shepherd's Tap Dancing School. Tap—where your feet hit the ground most of the time in heavy shoes—was the only kind of dancing I could ever do.

I hated—absolutely hated—how perfect the bodies of cheerleaders were. Cheerleaders had strong, silky thighs; I had skinny arms and legs and knobby knees. They had thick hair that curled—no, *coiled*—like gold wire, deep to the roots; I had soft, stringy hair that never kept a curl and was a hundred different colors (the dominant one my aunts called "dishwater blond"). They had pep and personality; I was shy. They had white front teeth, perfectly straight; I didn't. They never wore glasses; I wore thick lenses in rhinestone-studded blue aluminum frames that swept up like wings. Cheerleaders could do cartwheels all the way to school, if they wanted to; I was lucky to arrive unbroken each morning after stumbling on sidewalk cracks. They were born knowing how to flirt; I was born clueless. They had freckles; I had moles. They had boyfriends; I had pen pals in Germany.

Every season, to help celebrate a different sport, I sat in bleachers and watched boys juggling balls and girls bouncing onto fields or gym floors to cheer. *I* cheered too, of course. Well, in a way. The principal gave us pep talks about being sure the *whole school* supported its teams. Every Friday night a crowd of Golden Rams (*We are the Ra-ams! Mighty, mighty Ra-ams!*) cheered on Garfield High School's athletes. From the stands, I, too, shouted my lungs out.

Sometimes I got to be on the field. I was in the marching band for a while, but what adolescent boy wants to look at a girl dressed in band pants, gloves, a hard sixteen-inch hat with a silly white plume poking out the back, and a clarinet stuck in her mouth when he could stare at a real live cheerleader?

Wherever I sat or stood, I was always watching the cheerleaders, dreaming about being one. Or, when the dreams stopped for a while (as they did after every spring audition that I failed), imagining new ways I could ruin their lives.

And then, suddenly, I didn't hate cheerleaders anymore.

Over the decades that passed since my junior year, I sometimes wondered why my attitude had changed. These are the reasons I came up with: 1) I had become more mature and had learned to be more charitable to others, or, 2) I had at last come to my senses and realized that cheerleading was perhaps a waste of time (an early sign of my emerging feminism), or, 3) My powers of observation had improved, and I concluded that cheerleading was never going to be anything but a fantasy; the only way I would ever become a cheerleader or do a split was through surgery.

But I found something recently that has forced me to think about my transformation in another way. A way that's closer to the truth.

It was a picture from my high-school yearbook. My junior year. Although I had entirely forgotten the moment it records, when I looked at that photograph, the day rushed back to me. I remembered everything I felt, but now I also sensed its significance.

I'm facing a blackboard in the picture, scanning lines of poetry. All you can see is the back of my belted dress (hemline just below my knees), my white socks and Oxford shoes, two skinny calves, and a *very* skinny arm wildly marking iambs and anapests over John Masefield's "Sea-Fever." *I must go down to the seas again, to the lonely sea and the sky / And all I ask is a tall ship and a star to steer her by*. Those are the lines on the board. You can see only the backs of my classmates. They sit in rows of seats staring at me staring at the Masefield poem. It's a picture almost entirely of backs. A few students have their heads turned slightly, so you catch a little of their expression, if you look closely. Two boys are holding their chins in their hands and a third is yawning, covering his mouth. Or is he laughing?

It was the most exciting moment I had ever experienced in school.

But the *reason* for that excitement is what I need to clarify, and what it's taken me a long time to understand.

When I stood at the board, I was not aware at all that anyone else was in the room. Not the cheerleaders who were probably giggling at my skinny legs. Not the boys who had quickly tired of me, or the one laughing behind the back *I* had turned toward *him*. I was no longer aware of anyone because I was entirely lost in the white lines in front of me, and was happy being alone with them. It's not that I suddenly didn't care any longer about what the popular students thought of me. That's not why I turned my back, or what it meant. What you see in the picture is neither a realization nor a condemnation. It records no conscious act.

Instead, it shows the moment when I fell in love. For the first time in my life. The poem had overwhelmed me. Seduced me. I had never read such beautiful lines before, or heard the breath that hovers underneath them. I'd never experienced joy like that. I didn't know it then, but I would never be the same.

I must go down to the seas again, to the vagrant gypsy life.

My skinny, knobby knees were trembling hard as I sat down.

And that's the moment when I began to stop hating cheerleaders.

LINDA DYER

Votive

Being rural, we waited for the school bus in the dark early morning of daylight savings, then proceeded to the subdivisions. On our bus in 1972, it was unpopular to wear a "Vote McGovern" button, to carry a clarinet case, to read books on the ride. What a relief to focus on a battle outside the home, stand up for our man McGovern, believe the forces of liberal overspill would help out when Bobby Hawkins pushed you up against the graffiti wall and told you to take it back. *Take back McGovern. Say you vote Nixon.* All this for weeks of obsessive campaigning for something which might invade even our lone house with human kindness, bring us back to the fold, any fold—all of us too young to vote or influence our parents. Vindication was ours a few years later with "*I am not a crook*" and the guilty swaggering, a few convictions; but in the 70s, rural Oklahoma, we were commies and queers, relegated to sitting in the library again for the lunch hour, our brown bag lunches confiscated in the name of Nixon.

KATHY EVANS

After the Facts

Poetry and the Sophomores

I tell the students that writing is a moment of awareness. "Just go from the outer world to the inner world," I say. "Start here with the green of spring and the blossoms going wild along Sir Francis Drake Boulevard." But we are inside, and I don't mean the inner world. I mean, we are inside the portables while the high school is under siege by a construction crew on bulldozers. We're as hot and sticky as cotton candy. We're like a new form of trailer trash sitting at fake wood tables, in plastic chairs with metal legs, beige walls pocked with thumb tack holes, and one lonely *Animal Farm* poster. "What is Animal Farm anyway?" says one student to another. We're aliens. Some of the students put on their headphones; others look around distracted by what's truly in bud, the girl in the tube top, the seeds popping in the terrarium, or by the crows caw caw cawing in the sycamores. But some of them, surprisingly, stay focused like good little monks trying to save civilization. The small pubescent boy has his head down on the table near her long braceleted arm—an apple between them. This is the last hour of school, the last period of the day, the last rites in heat and spring, and who can blame them for slumping over like primates? I pledge to love the sophomores at any cost—their minds spinning like pinwheels; their own myths lived out not quite biblically; cell phones vibrating like small, trapped animals inside their pockets, purses, pouches; the instant messages showing up in secret codes in their own green mini-window—the blond in pink; the boy in the corner with hair that looks almost yanked out of his scalp. He goes on drumming on the table top with #2 Dixon pencils. He must be a drummer in a group called Flunked. "Hello out there," I say, "You who? This is Captain Poetry speaking. This is an air raid. Everyone drop to the floor like Keats. Get under your desks. Put your hands over your heads. Something is about to blow."

HENRY LOUIS GATES, JR.

from Colored People
A Memoir

It was Mama who took the battle to them, Mama who showed us how to fight. We didn't always win, of course. In eighth grade, my older brother Rocky couldn't be awarded West Virginia's most coveted prize for excellence in state history, a Golden Horseshoe, one of Daddy's white friends told us, because the hotel where we would have had to stay in the state capital was segregated. Hell, they'd just denied entry to Elgin Baylor, the star forward of the Minneapolis Lakers. Rocky had missed winning by "half a point," they said. He had misspelled a word, they said. Too bad, they said. Sometimes it seems Rocky's childhood ended that day, the day he found out why he had not won. Now, a Golden Horseshoe is the Nobel Prize of eighth graders in West Virginia. Your entire education had prepared you for this competition. Four winners per county. Meeting the governor. Fame. Glory.

One half point. A misspelled word. How it haunted Rocky! Then Elmer Shaver—the white man who was Daddy's boss at the phone company and one of his best friends—came up one night, late, and explained the whole thing in a whispered voice, while Rocky and I sat on our bunks in our bedroom, listening to John R. out of *Randy's Record Shop* in Gallatin, Tennessee. And then, after Mr. Shaver left, Mama tried to find the voice to tell it, to tell the awful truth of what those crackers did. How relieved Rocky was that it was not his fault, that he had not blown the chance of a lifetime to be the first colored Golden Horseshoe winner by transposing some letters.

But then, as soon as you let yourself feel relief, this next wave came crashing over you, larger and more dangerous than the first wave, of guilt and responsibility, and this wave was the terrible one, this wave crushing and inexorable: no matter what you did or how you did it, it didn't matter because it was their world, their sea, and their tide, and your little black ass was about as significant as a grain of yellow sand.

Something died inside, the part that spells the difference between hoping and doing, between casting wide or casting close, between wearing the horizon like a shawl around your shoulders or allowing it to choke you to death like one of those plastic dry cleaner's bags that warn of suffocation in dire blue letters. And something happened to Rocky when that county school board lied and told him that he had almost won, that he should have worked just a little harder, that he transposed two letters. That it could have happened to anyone, boy—but especially to you, *boy*.

I saw him nursing the injury in silence, unable to speak of it, unwilling to shed it. Paltry as it may seem from the vantage of adulthood, the knowledge of that deception cast a shadow over his life. That same knowledge drove me to win a Golden Horseshoe six years later.

Rocky kept tripping over those rules that you didn't know existed until you broke them. Like being selected in the eleventh grade by the school for Boys State, whereupon the white American Legion, led by Frank Price, informed the board that they preferred a white boy. Mr. Staggers, the principal, had to inform Frank Price that they'd take Paul Gates or send no one at all. He went, and we all rejoiced at another victory for the Negro race. But Rocky hurt from this sort of thing.

Rocky was five years and six grades ahead of me, so I tracked him through the school system quietly, stealthily, avoiding his pitfalls and false starts, emulating him but at a distance. It was a role I liked. The younger, the disciple, the pupil, the neophyte, the ephebe, the apprentice: that's a position people describe as one of confinement. To me, they have it exactly wrong. They don't see that it carries a kind of freedom: no anxiety about finding the path, just the determination to keep your feet on the path. Most of the time, I've found that challenge enough.

DIANE GILLIAM

Does Not Use Free Time Wisely

Color pictures 1 through 10 and underline the ones that start with F. Number 1 on the phonics paper is a fan, F. It's a lacy fan, so it should be white. It's shell-shaped, with lots of circle, triangle, thin oval shapes, and wavy line shapes drawn inside it for the lace. It's hard not to color in the air between the lace. The ladies at my grandma's church in West Virginia have fans, but they're cardboard, round-cornered squares on popsicle sticks, with pictures of blue-green and pink gardens and the names of funeral homes, or Jesus sitting on a big round rock with children. When I color in the air, I scrape it off with my thumbnail. The phonics fan would be for fancy ladies, ladies with white fluffy hair, not big ladies with false teeth and springy mixed black and gray hair rolled high in front and pinned in back like Grandma Novi's. For ladies with rings, not ladies with big hands and fat, wrinkled fingers. The phonics fan ends with a tiny ring to hold on to. I make my underline a little shorter than the circle, because that's how these fans are, they start big and get smaller and smaller.

Miss Sharp calls free time and I look for a long piece of white paper in the scrap box. I fold it accordion style, flip and fold, flip and fold, all the way to the end, to make a fan. I think how Grandma Novi rolls out pie crust with a glass and cuts it with a thin silver knife into strips, then she flips and folds the strips all under and over each other till she has a fancy design, like material with checks, on top of the purple blackberries. I hold some of my folds together and cut diamonds out of their edges, like when you make snowflakes; then I cut some hearts and some wavy peels. What else would be good for lace? It's allowed to walk around during free time, so I go over to the window and look for shapes in the weeds. You cut the shapes in halves, but they come out whole.

Miss Sharp calls my name to stay in at recess because I didn't finish my phonics paper. See now, she says, if you'd finished during phonics, or during free time, you could go out. I do the rest of my paper in one minute and give it to her. She gives me a sad face on it even though I didn't miss any, except for the fan. It doesn't count, Miss Sharp says, when you color things white, and she knows I tried to make the littlest underline I could just because I had to stay in. She says I have to put my head down till recess is over. I watch Miss Sharp over the corner of my elbow and think about Grandpa's porch swing high on the hill and about telling Miss Sharp how Grandma Novi could beat her up.

RICHARD HAGUE

from Milltown Natural
Essays and Stories from a Life

As a tight end, I made one great catch and one great run, and upon them I built, however unsteadily, my entire claim to understanding the deepest agendas of the sport. The catch was in a game against the St. Agnes team. It was a quick slant over the middle; I had to leap high to catch it; I was hit by what felt like a train in mid-air; I watched with interest as my own cleats revolved above me in slow motion against the reddish glow of the Mingo Junction sky, and I remember nothing after that except that I held on to the ball. This was decades before high-fives and spikes and other demonstrations; if any of us had dared to show any emotion, our coaches, Scooter Dugan and Paper Abramowicz, would have looked at us as if we were two-headed calves. My greatest satisfaction was that when I returned to the huddle I still had all of my teeth.

The run was an end-around, and it was against St. Stanislaus in a scrimmage at North End field, a dusty sink squeezed in between the neighborhood and the railroad at the foot of the old Panhandle Bridge into West Virginia. I took the handoff and ran like hell, and there was only one guy in front of me, the biggest kid on St. Stanislaus—I don't remember whether it was Mieczkowski or Kuzikowski—and I just put my shoulder down and ran right into him—and over him! Oh Lord, I had broken into the clear and I ran and ran, and vaguely, distantly behind me I heard a whistle blowing, and guys yelling, and after another twenty steps I stopped (there were no chalk lines to mark the end zone) and I looked back and saw all the St. Stanislaus guys spread across the field, and the coaches and my team all laughing. I had run clear past the end of the field, broken away, passed beyond. And as I trotted back, I relived in my thrilled flesh the crashing into my opponent, and his falling aside, and the rush of power in it. And I realized that the rush was as dangerous a thing as I'd ever felt except panic in my life, and I began to shy away from it, right there at the very moment of the experience, as one shies immediately away from a fire after being burnt. From that point, there on the dusty North End field, after a touchdown in a scrimmage, began my decline as a player. Though I continued to play football often and hard throughout my boyhood, that instinctive wariness of its power made of my play a kind of counterfeit, a sham.

But I did, after all, continue to compete: I had to. That was the rule. Boys in Steubenville played football, and if they didn't—well, it was almost unthinkable. What the hell *did* you do, if you didn't play football?

DAVID HASSLER

Wrestling Mr. Dietz

All during the winter of my seventh-grade year, I have a chronic cough and runny nose. But my father doesn't think I need to see a doctor. We've just spent two months talking to many different doctors and none of them was able to help my mother. My brother and I returned to school just two days after my mother's funeral. Now my father gives us pep talks, like a coach trying to encourage his team. "What doesn't kill you makes you stronger," he says. He writes this quote in red pen on a little piece of paper and tapes it to the lamp above his desk in his study at home. It is a quote from Nietzsche's *Twilight of the Idols*, one of his maxims from "life's school of war." I don't know this then, much less who Nietzsche is. But somehow after my mother's death, my brother and I are supposed to be stronger. It feels like wartime.

So I carry a box of Kleenex with me to school in my book bag. I blow my nose loudly in class, wanting the other students to laugh when they hear my loud honking. I don't think I am sick. My father tells me I am not really sick. "It's all in your head," he says. "Just grit your teeth, David, and ignore it."

Each morning, my father drops off my brother and me at the side doors of Davey Junior High, where, before school, a crowd of students sits in the cafeteria waiting for the first bell to ring. They slam their bags down on the tables and slump in plastic chairs, shouting and throwing wads of paper at each other. I always walk past them, up the stairs to Mr. Dietz's office on the second floor. No one ever asks me for a hall pass. I assume Mr. Dietz has told the monitors to let me go.

Mr. Dietz is my seventh-grade Life Science teacher and wrestling coach. Every morning I sit on his couch in his office where it is quiet and calm. Unlike my father's study at home, Mr. Dietz's shelves have very few books. Mostly, they are filled with beakers and scales, rolled-up charts and petri dishes, stacks of papers and mimeographs. Mr. Dietz has a large wooden desk with a scratched metal filing cabinet beside it. His old swivel chair squeaks when he leans back in it. I sit behind him on his orange and brown couch. Occasionally we'll talk about school or wrestling matches, but usually I just sit there quietly, watching him grade papers.

On the wrestling mats, Mr. Dietz teaches me reversals and escapes, how to hold my arms and legs out like a crab, scissor and trip my opponent. I don't remember ever pinning anyone. If I win a match, I win only by points. After practice, Mr. Dietz drives me home in his Ford Bronco, even though my house is on the other side of town.

Each night, I cannot go to sleep until I have finished all my school work, solved every math problem and read every page for Social Studies and English. I am determined to get straight A's. I spread my books out on the dining room table and lean over my pages. Some nights, worrying about a test the next day, I begin to cry. Then I feel my father's hands gripping my shoulders from behind. "It's good to cry," he says. "It's good to get it out of your system."

In school each morning, I am glad to sit again in Mr. Dietz's office before the first bell rings. We never talk about my mother or what it's like at home. I just sit there calmly and sink into the cushions of his couch, studying the curly red hairs on the back of his neck. One morning, by surprise, Mr. Dietz spins around from his desk and drops me to the floor, challenging me to a match. I laugh, feel his arms chafe against my face, smell his sweet and sour breath. He holds me in a full Nelson, waiting for me to escape, but I don't have the strength. I am happy to remain there, pinned in his embrace.

RUTH ELLA HENDRICKS

Professional Knowledge and Practice

This week it's testing and pressure and they send these police to oversee procedure. Make sure the teachers don't cheat. No student has an advantage. Check the principal, too. They walk around, important, glare, monitor and report violations, call down to the Board of Education, cover up that number line and cursive alphabet above the chalkboard. Use blank paper and tape.

Go in. Relieve a teacher. Provide a bathroom break. And the monitor says to me, *Don't be a distraction. All these charts must be covered now. Call the custodian. Get a ladder. This alphabet is considered a manipulative.* And I think, Huh? He's sent to stand high on a ladder, rustle paper, cut tape. Now. Right while students read and answer. I ask her where she is from. *The Superintendent's Office.* Cover up the alphabet letters? This is fifth grade. What possible aid—they might see an "A" or "B" or "C"? All of the above. The alphabet strips assist multiple choice? Quick conceal "Q." The small "z." Decisions made behind a mahogany desk in the stone mausoleum across from the museum. Or decided in the middle of the state. Everyone proficient by 2014. Last year testing discrepancies were labeled irregularities. Several teachers cited. And a principal received a plum. One, a lateral move just across the city. The other, a few months off, paid. So despite the patrol, someone, somewhere, is doing something irregular.

WILLIAM HEYEN

The End

In high school I won a football in a raffle. Katie Lee, sexy cheerleader, pushed it to me reluctantly Monday morning in Latin.

Painfully shy and feeling inferior, I hadn't attended the pep rally where "Stone" Cummings, team captain, had drawn my name from a trophy and asked, "Anybody know this Billy Hymen or whoever he is?"

Years later, I could order a meal from a waitress without blushing or becoming tongue-tied. I could kiss the woman who would become my wife and who would one day find, in a box of high school papers and yearbooks, a football signed by "Block" Patterson, "Snake" Lewis, "Zombie" Marko, "Bird" Leonard, and the Stone man himself.

That autumn of 1955 Stone and his teammates had battered the opposition into submission. Thirty years later, I propped the football on my mantle and looked at it in safety. . . . "The name of it is Time," says Robert Penn Warren in the last section of *Audubon: A Vision*. "But you must not pronounce its name. . . ."

Today, my intuitive twenty-year-old daughter took it down and flipped me a lateral across our living room. We ran outside for passes and punts. It was about time. I wonder where all those tough guys are now as my prize begins its postponed history of scrapes, lumps, protruding bladder, loose laces, its names spiraling all the way from high school and turning end over end to the end.

FAITH S. HOLSAERT

History Dancing

In the autumn of 1947, my mother took my four-year-old hand in hers and walked me three blocks to my first day at the Little Red School House, a three-story brick building in New York City's Greenwich Village. I have loved the promise of September mornings ever since.

We "fours" were taught by Sarah Abelson, a woman unfrighteningly close to us in height. Sixty years later, I remember placing my bean seed in a paper cup of soil and watching it emerge in science class; running and shouting in the autumn air of the rooftop playground with its brick lattice walls, where only we, the youngest students, were allowed. A timid child, I flourished on those days when the music teacher Charity Bailey led our piping voices in song, had us tumble on the classroom floor like Little Red Wagons. Charity summoned us one by one to strike a note on the piano. I stood beside the comfort of her presence, the keys at the level of my eyes, unable to disturb the air with a note. "Darling," she urged. "It won't bite." She pressed my pointer finger into an ivory key, the plinky tone eddying from my fingertip into a world which opened like a window to release my frail note into the autumn.

In kindergarten—the children's garden—I was infatuated with Charity as only a four-year-old can be. At the PTA meeting, my parents said, "Faith is crazy about you. She wants you to live with us." Charity asked, "Do you have a room?" She was commuting from Harlem, because no local landlord would rent to her, a black woman. My *children's garden* was sweet, but the real world of 1947 was not. My parents answered, "Yes," and Charity lived with us until my late teens.

Little Red was unabashedly a progressive school, bristling with postwar optimism and pride in its child-centered curriculum. My progressive parents *made* me wear blue jeans (called "dungarees" at the time), though I doggedly wore skirts over them. More substantively, we were not taught to read until we were seven; many children, and boys in particular, were not ready for reading at six, so we waited. Once we could read the *Dick and Janes*, we chose our reading texts from the bookshelves which lined our classrooms. Before the age of photocopy machines and internet search engines, our teachers crafted their curricula and assembled their own teaching materials. The Little Red School House differed in other ways, too. Some of the teachers had lost public school jobs because they had joined a teachers' union which McCarthy-era fervor had branded "Red." In the street, students at the nearby Our Lady of Pompeii Catholic School hissed not only "nigger lover" at my sister and me, but "Red. Little *Red*."

The autumn following the June 1953 executions of Julius and Ethel Rosenberg, my classmates and I entered the "tens," taught by Mimi Cooper Levy, a small-boned woman with a blazing smile and a dry wit. We studied electricity, human physiology, art, music, and Jewish History. We sat in a circle, with Mimi, like us, sitting on a child's chair while she told us what she knew. Studying spelling, we moved to sprawl on the floor, to play word games Mimi had invented: crosswords, fill-in-the-blanks, and rebuses. Compositions in our childish manuscripts filled the bulletin boards on three walls. We left those walls for the Metropolitan Museum to visit the Egyptians and afterward scuff our shoes in acrid autumn leaves.

Though we no longer played on the cloistered rooftop, with Mimi we felt happy and safe and adventurous. With Mimi and Charity, we wrote a December holiday play based on Sholom Aleichem's "Wise Men of Chelm" and performed it to school-wide acclaim. We returned from winter break primed for the spring of 1954. Rather than the alimentary canal and the nervous system, we would study human reproduction. We giggled. In social science we would move from Jewish History to what Mimi called Negro History. We didn't know what this was and perhaps neither did she that 1954 January. She opened with Crispus Attucks, a free black man, the first person to fall in the Revolutionary War.

In our circle, on breathless February mornings, the classroom hot and radiator-dry, we learned about Benjamin Banneker, the black man who completed the wheel-spoke design of Washington, DC. Afternoons, Mimi told us about the vagina and the penis. Mornings: slave ships and auction blocks. With Charity, we danced—mournful Isadora Duncans—to "Sometimes I Feel like a Motherless Child." Erections, wet dreams, budding breasts. Sojourner Truth. We went by subway to the Shomburg Library in Harlem. I checked out biographies of Harriet Tubman and John "Ossawatamie" Brown—figures whose intransigence fired my timid soul. Our improvised dance became "Go Down Moses." Sitting in our circle, we said *Dred Scott*—in 1857 the U.S. Supreme Court declared that he, as a black man, was not a citizen and had no right to sue for his freedom. With the brave and bleeding hearts of ten-year-olds we railed against the injustice. We opened our mouths and James Weldon Johnson's "Lift Every Voice and Sing" poured forth, but the next day we might be snaking through the classroom singing *Naa Naa Naa* and doing the Bunny Hop, a 1950s line dance.

Coincidentally, some girls were reading Nancy Drew (later exposed as racist by 1980s feminists), while others devoured horse books with that peculiar hunger of cement-locked city girls. My best friend received her first pair of knee-high nylons at Easter and there were playground murmurs of *training bras* and *camisoles*. Like other Village children, we walked our dogs, did our homework, borrowed books from the local public library, but unlike other children, we had one classmate whose unemployed father sat at home, raging at the Army-McCarthy hearings on the family television.

We followed Harriet Tubman and Frederick Douglass into the Civil War. Scorchingly, we asked, "How could our government call people *contraband*?" In Reconstruction glee, we danced syncopated to "Free at Last," though some grumbled they preferred the Lindy Hop. In 1898, *Plessy v. Ferguson* was decided by the U.S. Supreme Court. "Separate but Equal?" We were dumbstruck by the judicial setback, which reminded us: the father unemployed, Charity unable to rent an apartment, the Rosenbergs.

Mimi, teacher of spelling cards and talking circles and stories on walls, proposed we create a timeline of Negro history. In our final weeks, as it became warm enough to open classroom windows, warm enough to shed our unisex turtlenecks for shorter sleeves, and as I began to feel as if we'd already been expelled from Mimi's room, we assembled a pastiche of our own history reports (*Dred Scott, Plessy*) on lined paper, occasional newsprint photos like one of Mary McLeod Bethune shaking the hand of my mother's hero FDR, and newspaper articles, rising up and along the bulletin boards like latticed bricks, threaded into sequence by a heart line of crimson twine. We were embraced by these names and dates; we brimmed within them, entirely inhabiting them. With Langston Hughes, Jesse Owens, Jackie Robinson, Paul Robeson, and Ralph Bunche, our timeline reached the 1950s.

Our work was almost complete.

On May 18, 1954, Mimi handed coins to one of us. "Go get the *Times*. I think the desegregation case has been decided." One of us, perhaps a girl with thin braids down her back, ran into the May sunshine and around the corner. Within minutes, the metal fire door in the stairwell slammed open. Pounding up the stairs, she screamed, "We won."

Brown v. Board of Education had been decided.

Plessy had been struck down.

We spread the newspaper on the floor. We cut apart the columns of newsprint and glued them onto construction paper, before tacking them onto the bulletin board, completing the history which encircled us, *Brown* in its place, at the end of the red heart line. We rose to our feet. There was no sound in the "tens" room, just the external grate of the Italian coffee grinder three buildings down, the voices of sparrows, a bus accelerating up Sixth Avenue.

Mimi bumped her hip against one of ours. A girl hummed, *Naa Naa Naa Naa Na Na*. A boy grabbed me from behind. *Naa Naa Naa Naa Na Na*. We held one another, hands to still childish hips, flinging out one leg and then the other. Pen in hand, Phyllis Wheatley spun past as we jumped and panted below her. Feet out, feet in. *Contraband*. The Bunny Hop is a silly dance, jerking forward, back. *Naa Naa Naa Naa Na Na*. Langston Hughes and Marian Anderson. *Lift Every Voice and Sing*. We had to do that dance that afternoon, together jerking forward, together jumping back, weaving side to side over the floor where we had sprawled, moving forward, dancing, our teacher in the lead, her laugh fierce and her smile brilliant.

HANK HUDEPOHL

Friday Night Heroes

I remember the sound a collarbone makes when it snaps and the player's cry of agony just after. I've heard the pop of tendons in elbow and knee, and I've seen an arm dangle from a dislocated shoulder. I've watched as even the largest players on the field were carried off in stretchers, unable to move limbs or whole sections of their bodies, sometimes unable to utter their names.

Playing through a football season is a scenario of diminishing returns. You start with a whole thing, your healthy body, and little by little it comes apart. Some injuries happen suddenly, like a broken bone or a ruptured tendon, and it can end the season, while others wear on you: muscle aches, deep bruises, knee and ankle sprains that require constant taping for support. And injuries can carry over from one season to the next, or worse, can linger with a person into the deep recesses of a lifetime. By senior year, several of my classmates would never walk the same again due to knee injuries and subsequent surgeries.

For summer practice sessions, we'd meet twice a day, two hours in the morning until lunch and then two hours again in the afternoon. The practice field was a dust bowl that had earned the nickname Death Valley. It had spots of grass, but like the top of an aging man's head, the middle was bald earth and some green stubble of weeds and fescue lined the perimeter. On dry, summer afternoons, we'd stir up enough dust to cause us all to choke. At the end of the day, I'd spit and it would be the color of dirt. I'd wash out a black residue that had caked in the corners of my eyes in the shower afterward. During practice, we'd drink from a garden hose attached to a long, plastic pipe. The pipe had holes drilled in it at regular intervals like a flute. This way, about six of us could drink at the same time side by side. Gasping and sweating in ninety-degree heat, we'd suck down those little streams of water like a babe on a mother's breast, each of us with his mouth pressed to the pipe, swallowing as fast as the water would come to us.

At the beginning of the season, we had to cut our hair short—a buzz cut—and ride our bikes to practice, or else walk. We weren't supposed to be outside our houses after 8:30 P.M. Sometimes this presented a dilemma. I can remember being out late with my family—maybe we'd visited my grandparents, maybe we'd gone out to dinner or grocery shopping, some ordinary occasion—but I'd be out past curfew, so I'd have to crouch down in the back seat of the car like a convict while we drove through town back home. Some players broke rules blatantly, staying up well into the night, swallowing Budweiser or Schlitz or whatever cans of beer they could empty down their throats. Looking back, I suspect that more than a few of my classmates were alcoholics by the age of sixteen, having begun their bingeing as early as fifth grade. But that was not the norm. The high school tradition was a winning one, so people sacrificed eagerly for it. Friday night football games attracted most of the community, and it was here that kids began to worship their high school stars. It seemed obvious to me during those autumn evenings, with all eyes on the field, that the only way to be alive was to be just like those players in blue and white.

I used to catch footballs like my life depended on it, and to some extent, it did. I was young and trying to make a name for myself, seeking out my limits. I lived for the pure moment of tracking an airborne ball on a full sprint, running under it, catching the ball without breaking stride, tucking it away under my arm. The flight of the ball is a journey of silence. When the quarterback throws a high-arching pass downfield, the crowd, too, is elevated and moves through the air. Our world becomes the spinning ball. The arc of a long pass has the same grace of flight as a celestial body; the laws of the universe hold true both on and off the field. The forward pass is the game's moment of transcendence; it is the vertical direction, the z-axis, the third dimension. The flight of a pass enacts the thrill of a momentary release from our selves, which is, as Robert Frost noted in a poem called "Birches," "good both going and coming back." Surprisingly, the forward pass wasn't part of the game's original design. But the act of throwing an object at a target downfield was not a twentieth-century invention. It is, in fact, an archetypal experience: the stone that is launched from a sling, the spear that finds its prey, the arrow that is shot through the apple. We have always delighted in convergence, and we watch falling stars with wonder.

The purest catch is the diving catch—when, at the very last instant, you leave your feet in a forward lunge and, with outstretched arms, snare the nose of the ball with your fingertips. The trick is to hang onto the ball as you belly-whop against the ground. I used to stay after practice to catch pass after pass. Other players had showered and gone home before I came off the field. I never tired of the thrill; the last catch felt as miraculous to me as the day's first. One particular coach—to whom I am greatly indebted—stayed, throwing deep passes to me with the nonchalance of someone tossing stones into a river.

Game night was every player's chance to make it big in the community. But ambition made the game complex, the friendships spiteful, the team politics ugly. Parents wanted to know, and now, why isn't my son playing? I had a starting role, but I sometimes questioned the intentions of my teammates. Were they secretly hoping I'd be maimed? George Orwell voiced a similar bout of apprehension, when, in "The Sporting Spirit," he said, "Serious sport has nothing to do with fair play. It is bound up with hatred, jealousy, boastfulness, disregard of all rules and sadistic pleasure in witnessing violence: in other words it is war minus the shooting." His account may be a shade more sinister than my experience, but exaggeration sprouts from the seed of truth. The plain truth was this: if you practiced as much football as we did, you didn't want to watch the game from the sideline. You wanted a piece of the glory.

When people talk about their glory days, many seem to reference the competitions of their youth. Napoleon once said, "Glory is fleeting, but obscurity is forever." Glory, or in the Greek sense, *kleos*, is the hero's quest: remembrance, immortality. The notion of glory was much less grand for me and for other boys, but no less palpable. We just wanted to make something of ourselves. For one of the very first times in our lives, all attention was on us. The field was a stage where we could win the day in the name of our high school or even our whole town, or maybe, at the very least, in the name of our family. The school's long tradition of winning state championships suggested that we could do it again, and the town needed a legendary win every time the game clock ticked. Some of the townspeople expected us, I think, to return them to their youth at the expense of ours. Tradition is inextricable from the price it exacts.

I saw players with a body for the game and not the heart. This was anguish, especially for our coaches, but it was not as hard for me to watch as the players with the heart for it but not the body. These boys threw their thin bodies into the line of scrimmage like a death wish. In a sense, we are all colliding with our fate, some of us more courageously than others. Like most, I sometimes look back into my past for answers to my present. But history is not a straight line. I consider my high school days, the friends I knew, and the games I played. Sometimes, things actually do become clearer as I grow older. Other times, I'm less certain. But as my body ages, my desire to make the spectacular catch has not left me. And it has nothing to do with pleasing the crowds: give me an empty stadium. I wonder about this, why I still feel its pull, why it is part of me. Perhaps age leads us to cherish beauty in all her forms. Maybe I'm still drawn to it because I think of the completed pass as an affirmation of life and an act of beauty, not just a longing for it.

LAWSON FUSAO INADA

Our Song

> It was early one Monday morning,
> And I was on my way to school . . . —
> —*Big Joe Turner,* "Wee Baby Blues"

It was morning recess—Lincoln School, Fresno, California, 1946—when Shigeru Konishi began calling Alfredo Marquez "T-Bone," because of the lyrics Alfredo was repeatedly singing. The bell rang, we went back to class, but the name stuck: "T-Bone."

It all happened naturally: a kid from American concentration camps renaming a Mexican classmate from the projects after the African-American blues master, "T-Bone" Walker. We knew the music, and our teacher didn't. That was the beauty of it.

The music resided in our resident jukeboxes, whereas the teachers arrived daily from across the tracks, that town of different music, as played on all their radio stations. And although, or because, this was California, visible and visceral boundaries were in place. We had our foods, our musics, and they had theirs.

We also had our languages, and the teachers continually attempted to correct our pronunciation—what they called our "accents." School, then, was somewhat of a "correctional institution," and incorrect language was cause for punishment. But the likes of "T-Bone" Walker, Big Joe Turner, and Sister Rosetta Tharpe were not to be corrected; rather, they belted out their songs, their language, loud, and kept on doing it.

So there was school, and there were our jukeboxes—our West Fresno libraries. And unlike drab classrooms with tattered textbooks, jukeboxes were colorful and full of *now*; the music was magnetic, it drew us in with gravity, then sent us spinning outward with centrifugal force, beyond China Alley, the Buddhist temple, beyond the bars, labor buses, patrolling police wagons, beyond the projects, labor camps, vineyards, cotton-fields, and certainly beyond the schools to the world where glorious things were happening. But how to get there?

Schooling was schooling, or else, and elder guys in the neighborhood could go into the military, but by the time we matriculated into high school, the music matriculated (or was permitted, or was not to be denied) directly into the auditorium for talent assemblies, where singers could "be" Ruth Brown, Billie Holiday, the Clovers, and guys like Shigeru and "T-Bone" could "blow" in a group alongside Cleophas and Napoleon, playing compositions by a Lester Young, a Charlie Parker . . . And things were happening elsewhere: "protests," and after Jackie Robinson, Mike Garcia was pitching for the Indians.

In our senior year, Sam Jones and I were chosen by teachers to select our class song. The standard "Look for the Silver Lining," was deemed acceptable. But the way we sang it at graduation, unbeknownst to the teachers, was straight out of the jukebox—as performed by trumpeter Chet Baker. The alma mater didn't do much, but our song swung!

JULIA SPICHER KASDORF

Portrait of a Poet as a Public School Kid

The year I discovered poetry, trade embargoes stranded the grown-ups in gas lines. Our rural school district closed my oil-burning junior high and ran double sessions in an older building still heated with coal. For several winter months, I rose at five to ride a bus for an hour to the other junior high, where we seemed always lost in the hallways and short of time. With all seven class periods crammed into four hours, a full day passed in a blur before lunchtime. I don't recall one teacher or one thing they taught us that year, although I can now guess that among the lost subjects were algebra and American history.

My only memory from that time concerns a man named Gar Bethel. About him, I recall everything: camel corduroy blazer with suede elbow patches, blue jeans, a slight limp, a shock of curly reddish-blond hair, and a deep, gentle voice. He read a poem about oranges with leather skins and said, "Why not think up an orange with leather skin . . . why not think of a square orange with leather skin . . . or a whole crate of them?"

This truly shocked us, children already becoming as flat-footed and pragmatic as our parents, that brutal season. In one gesture, he invited us to find our imaginations and gave us permission to make no sense or to invent a new kind of sense altogether. In my memory, he met with our English class every day for two weeks, but with some research, I was amazed to discover that we met for only four abbreviated class periods.

On Gar Bethel's last day, I handed him a long poem I'd written about my father. That summer, my English teacher showed me my poem printed in *Images Remembered*, a perfect-bound paperback of student writing collected from 140 elementary and secondary schools that had participated in the Pennsylvania poets-in-the-schools program during the academic year 1975–1976. Represented were schools from Philadelphia and Pittsburgh and also those invisible towns like my own in between: Oil City and Homer City, Tyrone and Altoona.

I was so surprised to see my words in a book that I wept after the teacher left, bewildered by my own response. I have never since been so moved by a success. Then I stretched out on the living room floor as if I'd been flattened by something miraculous. Gar Bethel, a man with an angelic-sounding name, a man who wrote poems, thought that art was as important as money or the war I'd grown up watching on TV, and somewhere adults cared enough to make a real book of kids' writing—not just purple mimeographed sheets—and a teacher had driven all the way to my house just to deliver that book in the middle of August! I began to think of myself as a writer that day.

When I got to ninth grade, tests sorted us into tracked classes for senior high. Although I had become a reader and writer of some passion, atrocious spelling scores on a standardized test excluded me from the top English classes. So, I joined that vast herd of students who are neither exceptionally bright nor exceptionally dim. In senior high, again riding nearly an hour to school each morning, I watched many of my bus mates drop out, do drugs, blow up school toilets with M-80s, or just grow dull and sullen, mere numbers in a class that began with more than 1,000 and graduated 806. On land that had once been a family farm, our consolidated school sprawled like a factory or prison ringed with chain-link fence and flanked by parking lots and a giant football stadium. Poets-in-the-schools no longer fit into the budget, I was told, though I knew there were funds enough to buy contact lenses for starting football players.

But during the summer between my junior and senior years, I attended the Pennsylvania Governor's School for the Arts. In five intense weeks, I saw my first opera, learned how to throw a clay pot, and wrote all the time, completing a new draft or revision of a poem every day. I was still a self-conscious scribbler, but an ingredient greater than hard work transformed skeletons of abstract words into poems about actual experience and emotion, verse that was truly free. The metamorphosis had something to do with poet Deborah Burnham, who still teaches in the program, and with teenagers who were as passionate about melodies or colors or dance steps as I was about words. And no one called us nerds.

After Governor's School, returning to a high school that seemed to exist mostly to support a winning football team, I organized a literary magazine and pulled up my grades so that I was inducted into the National Honor Society late in my senior year. That fall, I voted in my first, disappointing national election, and on a class trip to Harrisburg, I pleaded with legislators to recognize the importance of Governor's School. Many other alumni did the same. Not only had the program educated young artists, it had created citizens—on the eve of a decade that would see vicious attacks on public funding for the arts at the national level and the obliteration of many local arts education programs.

A few years ago, I came across a poem by Gar Bethel in *Prairie Schooner* and wrote to him in care of the journal. Yes, he replied, he recalled teaching eighth-graders that cold winter of economic recession and no gas in western Pennsylvania; he was a migrant worker that season, traveling between motels and strange public school classrooms. Gar now lives and writes in Kansas, but poets-in-the-schools patched him through a tough time. Examining the *Images Remembered* anthology, I recognize the names of many of the young poets who'd been employed by the state to visit public schools that year. One went on to teach in the MFA program at Sarah Lawrence College; one is the editor of a national poetry journal; one edits the poetry series at Carnegie Mellon University Press; one received the National Poetry Series Award a few years back. One is my editor at the University of Pittsburgh Press; and one, who retired from teaching at the distinguished Iowa Writers' Workshop, wrote an endorsement for my first book.

As a child, I could have never guessed that those four brief class periods, which salvaged a dreary year and bloomed vividly into two weeks in my memory, could have been as life-sustaining for those visiting poets as they were for me. How many children's lives are changed by writing poetry, I cannot say. There are no tests for that. And while creative writing did not cure my spelling problems instantly, that handicap simply vanished in time, replaced by a desire to read and write well. Moreover, learning to use my imagination has enabled me to care about people and communities beyond my own. Writing and reading poetry—and now teaching it—continue to build my character and enlarge my heart. None of this would have happened without public funding for the arts. I count it a stroke of grace or luck that such funding was always there for me—but just barely—and I wonder who will surprise public school kids with their own possibilities now, as gas prices continue to rise, during another war.

GARRISON KEILLOR

from "School"

School started the day after Labor Day, Tuesday, the Tuesday when my grandfather went, and in 1918 my father, and in 1948 me. It was the same day, in the same brick schoolhouse, the former New Albion Academy, now named Nelson School. The same misty painting of George Washington looked down on us all from above the blackboard, next to his closest friend, Abraham Lincoln. Lincoln was kind and patient and we looked to him for sympathy. Washington looked as if he had a headache. His mouth was set in a prim, pained expression of disapproval. Maybe people made fun of him for his long, frizzy hair, which resembled our teacher's, Mrs. Meiers's, and that had soured his disposition. She said he had bad teeth—a good lesson for us to remember: to brush after every meal, up and down, thirty times. The great men held the room in their gaze, even the back corner by the windows. I bent over my desk, trying to make fat vowels sit on the line like fruit, the tails of consonants hang below, and colored the maps of English and French empires, and memorized arithmetic tables and state capitals and major exports of many lands, and when I was stumped, looked up to see George Washington's sour look and Lincoln's of pity and friendship, an old married couple on the wall. School, their old home, smelled of powerful floor wax and disinfectant, the smell of patriotism.

Mine was a vintage desk with iron scrollwork on the sides, an empty inkwell on top, a shelf below, lumps of petrified gum on the underside of it and some ancient inscriptions, one from '94 ("Lew P.") that made me think how old I'd be in '94 (fifty-two) and wonder who would have my place. I thought of leaving that child a message. A slip of paper stuck in a crack: "Hello. September 9, 1952. I'm in the fifth grade. It's sunny today. We had wieners for lunch and we played pom-pom-pullaway at recess. We are studying England. I hope you are well and enjoy school. If you find this, let me know. I'm 52 years old. . ."

I liked Mrs. Meiers a lot, though; she was a plump lady with bags of fat on her arms that danced when she wrote on the board: we named them Hoppy and Bob. That gave her a good mark for friendliness in my book, whereas Miss Conway of fourth grade struck me as suspiciously thin. What was her problem? Nerves, I suppose. She bit her lips and squinted and snaked her skinny hand into her dress to shore up a strap, and she was easily startled by loud noises. Two or three times a day, Paul or Jim or Lance would let go with a book, dropping it flat for maximum whack, and yell, "Sorry, Miss Conway!" as the poor woman jerked like a fish on the line. It could be done by slamming a door or dropping the window, too, or even scraping a chair, and once a loud slam made *her* drop a stack of books, which gave us a double jerk. It worked better if we were very quiet before the noise. Often, the class would be so quiet, our little heads bent over our work, that she would look up and congratulate us on our excellent behavior, and when she looked back down at her book, *wham!* and she did the best jerk we had ever seen. There were five classes of spasms: The Jerk, The Jump, The High Jump, The Pants Jump, and The Loopdeloop, and we knew when she was prime for a big one. It was after we had put her through a hard morning workout, including several good jumps, and a noisy lunch period, and she had lectured us in her thin weepy voice, then we knew she was all wound up for the Loopdeloop. All it required was an extra effort: *throwing* a dictionary flat at the floor or dropping the globe, which sounded like a car crash. . . .

Mrs. Meiers had a Reading Club on the bulletin board, a sheet of brown wrapping paper with a border of book jackets, our names written in her plump firm hand and after each name a gold star for each book read, but she has given it up because some names have so many stars. Her good readers are voracious and read their weight in books every week, while the slow readers lag behind. Daryl Tollerud has read two books, Mary Mueller has read sixty-seven, and her stars are jammed in tight behind her name. In the encyclopedia, I'm up to Customs of Many Lands and she is up to

Volcanoes. She is the queen of Reading Club and she knows it. Girls want to sit next to her at lunch. Donna Bunsen is second with forty-six. Her close friends believe that Mary writes her book reports from book jackets. *Look at this: "Little House on the Prairie* is a book about the Ingalls family living in South Dakota . . ." *She didn't read that book, the big cheater*. Marilyn Peterson put a slip of paper in a book in Mary's desk. It said, "You big cheater"; she put it in at the end of the book. Mary didn't say anything about it. "See?" Marilyn said. "She didn't read that book."

It took me a long time to learn to read. I was wrong about so many words. *Cat, can't. Tough, through, thought. Shinola*. It was like reading a cloud of mosquitoes. . . .

One word I liked was *popular*. It sounded good, it felt good to say, it made lights come on in my mouth. I drew a rebus: a bottle of Nu-Grape + U + a Lazy Ike. *Pop-u-lure*. It didn't occur in our reading book, where little children did the right thing although their friends scoffed at them and where despised animals wandered alone and redeemed themselves through pure goodness and eventually triumphed to become Top Dog, The Duck of Ducks, The Grand Turtlissimo, The Greatest Pig Of Them All, which, though thrilling, didn't appeal to me so much as plain *popular*. "The popular boy came out the door and everybody smiled and laughed. They were so glad to see him. They all crowded around him to see what he wanted to do."

Morning and afternoon, school recessed and we took to the playground; everyone burst out the door except me. Mrs. Meiers said, "Don't run! Walk!" I always walked. I was in no hurry. I knew what was out there. The girls played in front. Little girls played tag and stoop-ball, hopscotch, skipped rope; big girls sat under the pine tree and whispered. Some girls went to the swings. Boys went out back and played baseball, except for some odd boys who lay around in the shade and fooled with jackknives and talked dirty. I could go in the shade or stand by the backstop and wait to be chosen. Daryl and David always chose up sides and always chose the same people first, the popular ones. . . . They took their sweet time choosing us, we had plenty of time to study our shoes. Mine were Keds, black, though white ones were more popular.

Mother said black wouldn't show dirt. She didn't know how the wrong shoes could mark a person and raise questions in other people's minds. "Why do you wear black tennis shoes?" Daryl asked me once. He had me there. I didn't know. I guessed I was just that sort of person, whether I wanted to be or not.

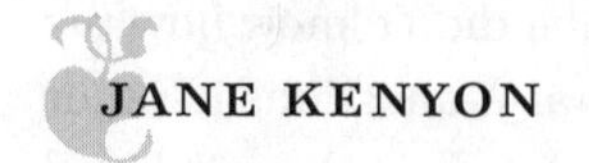

JANE KENYON

Dreams of Math

With trepidation I've glanced over the school-bus schedules in the *Monitor* these last few days. Something in me, and I suspect in many of us, still thinks that *they* are going to appear from nowhere to make me go shopping with Mother for books and pencils, then to force me back into the classroom.

The same strange forces robbed me of countless hours wasted on dusty school buses. How well I remember standing in the September morning fog, waiting for the yellow bulk of the school bus to appear out of white air. We could hear the bus long before the twin blinking lights rose to the top of Foster Road and the door swung open.

Though I'm twenty-five years and almost a thousand miles away from my public education, I still dream that I'm lost in the hallways of a school, looking for a locker, which, once found, I cannot open because I have forgotten the combination. Everybody must endure these nightmares about being late, lost, unprepared, and altogether lacking the "pitch and merit" of a successful seventh grader.

How many times have I dreamt that the season for final exams has come, and I go dutifully from room to room taking my tests. But what's this? It seems I have a test in physics, a class in which I have forgotten I was enrolled, and which I have neglected to attend all semester. It is the spring term of my senior year.

Like Keats's sufferer in "La Belle Dame Sans Merci," I awaken "on the cold hillside." My heart races as I begin to plead my case. It's no good—I can't fill a physics blue book with poetry.

Trouble, trouble. Why is there no happy moment in these dreams of school? I guess it's because to be in school was to be anxious, at least for me. I felt liable for the things I didn't know. I must have thought I should be like the last polymath, who lived in the eighteenth century.

The school I attended from kindergarten through grade four was a one-room country school on the outskirts of Ann Arbor, Michigan. The small, white clapboard building, complete with large bell, hunkered with its flagpole and swing sets in the midst of small farms and apple orchards not far from the Huron River. One teacher taught all the grades, so that our fates were sealed with Miss Irwin's for as long as Miss Irwin lasted at Foster School #16 Fractional.

We began our day with the salute to the flag, under Gilbert Stuart's classic portrait of George Washington. From there we went on to lessons and lunch, then took naps with our heads down on our desks. We ended the day with square dancing. Miss Irwin was free to set the tone in any way she chose.

Much as I loved the dancing, I had trouble elsewhere early in my schooling. I had math anxiety, as it's come to be called. Letters, reading, spelling made sense to me, but numbers had such strange proclivities. That zero times four was zero, canceling the existence of the four, seemed dubious at best.

As I advanced through the higher grades, which took me, eventually, into the Ann Arbor public schools—there were four in my kindergarten and nine hundred in my graduating senior class—my math anxiety multiplied, so to speak. Even geometry, which my friends told me I'd be able to master, bollixed me. In college I avoided math and science whenever possible. I turned to arts and letters, where I felt on safer ground.

It troubled me throughout my education that I had to obey and perform for teachers whose judgment I didn't respect. I had a few teachers whom I respected enormously, a middling group of ordinary mortals, and finally an index of teachers I thought ill of, who nonetheless had the power to determine the course of my education and my life.

High school history, for example, was taught as an endless series of wars. When I got to the university and encountered social and intellectual history, the history that lives and breathes, I felt all the more resentful of my earlier training.

Our schooling makes us brave or timid, adept socially or not; it makes us team players or selfish players. Children may understand the larger implications of their classes long before they can articulate their feelings. So remember, when you urge your children to hurry lest they miss the bus, you urge them toward a complicated future, much of which is subject to random luck.

JESSE LEE KERCHEVAL

from "Everything You Always Wanted to Know"

OCTOBER 1970, COCOA, FLORIDA

One Saturday, my sister Carol and her best friend, Stephanie, marched into the mall bookstore and bought a paperback copy of *Everything You Always Wanted to Know about Sex but Were Afraid to Ask.* They let everyone they knew at Cocoa High sign up for a turn with the book. Everybody but me.

All I knew was that suddenly everyone at school was laughing at things I didn't find funny, telling jokes I didn't get. Then on Friday, Carol came up to me in the lunch room during fourth period begging for my help. Carol had been supposed to pass the book to Pete Orsini but had left it in her desk in Madame Muller's classroom. Madame Muller was our French teacher, a woman who steadfastly refused to admit that there were French names for parts of the body. Stephanie, Carol said, would kill her when she found out she'd lost the book, not to mention Pete. Since I had French III next period, it was up to me, her only sister, to save her.

"You can do it," she said.

I stood with my arms crossed. "Why should I?" I said, upset she'd left me out of the only illicit thing she'd ever done in her life.

Carol sighed. "I'll let you read the book."

I nodded. "Deal."

"It's under the third seat from the door," she said, leaving me with a firm squeeze of my shoulder.

It wasn't easy to get away with sitting at a different desk in a class that had only four bored inmates. But I did it, making a show of finding gum stuck to my usual seat and moving to the one where Carol said she'd sat. Then I waited until the lights were off and Madame Muller was showing French Impressionist slides.

In the dim light, I slumped down in the desk, groping among the old gum and papers for the book. "Camille Pissarro's *Place du Théâtre Français*, painted in 1898," Madame Muller read from the booklet that came with the slides. "Notice the panorama of blurred dark figures against a light background." The slide projector clicked. A fuzzy scene of a street full of people and wagons appeared. My fingers found the book, closed around it. I slipped it out of the desk and into my lap. Madame Muller went on, reading the description of the next painting before she changed slides, "Édouard Manet's *Déjeuner sur l'Herbe*, painted in 1863. Notice the combination of a modern setting with traditional sixteenth-century Italian themes." Carol and Stephanie had ripped off the real jacket and recovered the book with yellow-and-orange flowered contact paper, and Magic Markered *Betty Crocker's Hot Dishes* on the spine, another joke I didn't get. "Contemporary viewers," Madame Muller said, "found the portrayal of a nude woman and two clothed men shocking." *Click, FLASH*. The screen was blank, and the flood of light made me sit up, afraid of getting caught.

Madame went on. "Edgar Degas's *Ballet Rehearsal (Adagio)*, painted in 1876. Notice his use of arrested motion," she said, and *click*, some leaping ballerinas appeared very like ones I remembered from my third-grade tour of the National Art Museum. I pretended to be interested in the blurry, bluish montage of tutus and toe shoes. "Edgar Degas's *The Morning Bath*," she announced, and *click*, there was another bright, empty blank. Stephen, the only boy in the class, raised his hand. Stephen was president of the French Club (a true losers' organization) and the only student with any enthusiasm left for French after three years of Madame Muller. The rest of us sincerely wished we had taken Spanish.

"Pardon, Madame," Stephen said, rolling his "r." "There isn't any picture on the screen."

"Of course not, Stephen," murmured Madame Muller, pronouncing his name with a soft "ph" in the middle, which suited Stephen, so soft and plump, too well. "I would *never* show *nudes* in mixed company."

So she went on, showing or not showing us the Impressionist masters. When a blank screen gave me enough light to read, I flipped open the book. *Breasts are erotic . . .*

Then a landscape came on, and I lost my place in the gloom. *Click, FLASH*. More light. *The size of the penis does not . . .*

Three dim landscapes in a row, and I fumbled. We were moving on, she announced, to the Postimpressionists. "Paul Cézanne's *La Montagne Sainte-Victoire,*" Madame Muller droned, "notice the . . . " *Click, FLASH.* We got back to more censored nakedness. By the light of Madame Muller's invisible nudes, I caught my first knee-weakening glimpses of the words *penis, vagina*, and *orgasm*. My tiny nipples sat up in the padded bomb shelters of my bra and begged.

BARBARA KINGSOLVER

How Mr. Dewey Decimal Saved My Life

A librarian named Miss Truman Richey snatched me from the jaws of ruin, and it's too late now to thank her. I'm not the first person to notice that we rarely get around to thanking those who've helped us most. Salvation is such a heady thing the temptation is to dance gasping on the shore, shouting that we are alive, till our forgotten savior has long since gone under. Or else sit quietly, sideswiped and embarrassed, mumbling that we really did know pretty much how to swim. But now that I see the wreck that could have been, without Miss Richey, I'm of a fearsome mind to throw my arms around every living librarian who crosses my path, on behalf of the souls they never knew they saved.

I reached high school at the close of the sixties, in the Commonwealth of Kentucky, whose ranking on educational spending was I think around fifty-first, after Mississippi and whatever was below Mississippi. Recently Kentucky has drastically changed the way money is spent on its schools, but back then, the wealth of the county decreed the wealth of the school, and few coins fell from the money trees that grew in Lexington. Our county, out where the bluegrass begins to turn brown, was just scraping by. Many a dedicated teacher served out earnest missions in our halls, but it was hard to spin silk purses out of a sow's ear budget. We didn't get anything fancy like Latin or Calculus. Apart from English, the only two courses of study that ran for four consecutive years, each one building upon the last, were segregated: Home Ec for girls and Shop for boys. And so I stand today, a woman who knows how to upholster, color-coordinate a table setting, and plan a traditional wedding—valuable skills I'm still waiting to put to good use in my life.

As far as I could see from the lofty vantage point of age sixteen, there was nothing required of me at Nicholas County High that was going to keep me off the streets; unfortunately we had no streets, either. We had lanes, roads, and rural free delivery routes, six in number, I think. We had two stoplights, which were set to burn green in all directions after 6 P.M. so as not, should the event of traffic arise, to slow anybody up.

What we *didn't* have included almost anything respectable teenagers might do in the way of entertainment. In fact, there was one thing for teenagers to do to entertain themselves, and it was done in the backs of Fords and Chevrolets. It wasn't upholstering skills that were brought to bear on those backseats, either. Though the wedding-planning skills did follow.

I found myself beginning a third year of high school in a state of unrest, certain I already knew what there was to know, academically speaking—all wised up and no place to go. Some of my peers used the strategy of rationing out the science and math classes between periods of suspension or childbirth, stretching their schooling over the allotted four years, and I envied their broader vision. I had gone right ahead and used the classes up, like a reckless hiker gobbling up all the rations on day one of a long march. Now I faced years of study hall, with brief interludes of Home Ec III and IV as the bright spots. I was developing a lean and hungry outlook.

We did have a school library, and a librarian who was surely paid inadequately to do the work she did. Yet there she was, every afternoon, presiding over the study hall, and she noticed me. For reasons I can't fathom, she discerned potential. I expect she saw my future, or at least the one I craved so hard it must have materialized in the air above me, connected to my head by little cartoon bubbles. If that's the future she saw, it was riding down the road on the back of a motorcycle, wearing a black leather jacket with "Violators" (that was the name of our county's motorcycle gang, and I'm not kidding) stitched in a solemn arc across the back.

There is no way on earth I really would have ended up a Violator Girlfriend—I could only dream of such a thrilling fate. But I was set hard upon wrecking my reputation in the limited ways available to skinny, unsought-after girls. They consisted mainly of cutting up in class, pretending to be surly, and making up shocking, entirely untrue stories about my home life. I wonder now that my parents continued to feed me. I clawed like a cat in a gunnysack against the doom I feared: staying home to reupholster my mother's couch one hundred thousand weekends in a row, until some tolerant myopic farm boy came along to rescue me from sewing-machine slavery.

Miss Richey had something else in mind. She took me by the arm in study hall one day and said, "Barbara, I'm going to teach you Dewey Decimal."

One more valuable skill in my life.

She launched me on the project of cataloging and shelving every one of the, probably, thousand books in the Nicholas County High School library. And since it beat Home Ec III by a mile, I spent my study-hall hours this way without audible complaint, so long as I could look plenty surly while I did it. Though it was hard to see the real point of organizing books nobody ever looked at. And since it was my God-given duty in those days to be frank as a plank, I said as much to Miss Richey.

She just smiled. She with her hidden agenda. And gradually, in the process of handling every book in the room, I made some discoveries. I found *Gone with the Wind*, which I suspected my mother felt was kind of trashy, and I found Edgar Allan Poe, who scared me witless. I found that the call number for books about snakes is 666. I found William Saroyan's *Human Comedy*, down there on the shelf between Human Anatomy and Human Physiology, where probably no one had touched it since 1943. But I read it, and it spoke to me. In spite of myself I imagined the life of an immigrant son who believed human kindness was a tangible and glorious thing. I began to think about words like *tangible* and *glorious*. I read on. After I'd read all the good ones, I went back and read Human Anatomy and Human Physiology and found that I liked those pretty well too.

It came to pass in two short years that the walls of my high school dropped down, and I caught the scent of a world. I started to dream up intoxicating lives for myself that I could not have conceived without the books. So I didn't end up on a motorcycle. I ended up roaring hell-for-leather down the backroads of transcendent, reeling sentences. A writer. Imagine that.

LEONARD KRESS

Yearbook

Lonnie, Lonnie, no one in my suburban high school didn't love you. Your blond smile and your black, juice-can curled hair. Your lacrosse legs, not knock-kneed and never scraped like the others'. Your cheers always delivered in perfect pleated pitch, pep-rally queen, drama club lead, student council head, so much more than pep and pompoms. Lonnie, Lonnie, no one didn't love you, students, teachers, administrators, secretarial and cafeteria staff, custodians. No clique would dare to claim you for its own. First invited to all parties, even newly transferred city kids (all smokes and sass and badinage) lost it when you passed them in the hall, slipping into bathrooms to recalibrate their cool. Lonnie, Lonnie, no one didn't love you, unanimous Queen—Homecoming, Harvest, Prom, always with a different date. You never ever broke those rules you had no say in making. Debating whiz, Junior Miss, Merit Scholar. No, not even to rail against that tumor, Lonnie, voted even more likely than you to succeed. That tumor that midway through your junior year crowded out your brain. A PET scan now would show it giving its all, exploding in spirit and glory, sporting the school colors, red and blue.

STEPHEN KUUSISTO

from Planet of the Blind

By the age of five, I've been in and out of hospitals. The muscles around my eyes have been cut and stitched as a means of correcting my strabismus. After the surgery I have bandages on my eyes for several months, and that is when I learn to hear. I spend whole afternoons listening. I can hear the wooden gears of the railroad clock that hangs on the far wall.

The strabismus operation has made me appear less cross-eyed, though the eyes move independently, and in their separate depths of color they afford me nothing like depth perception or balance. By now my glasses are extremely thick. They allow me to make use of my delicate residual vision, but they're cumbersome and painful to wear, and the target of teasing by other children.

On the first day of school the teacher, Mrs. Edinger, posts a photograph above the blackboard; two chubby infants swaddled in diapers stare down on the class. Those who are caught whispering will have their names appended under the babies' curled feet.

"This is the Baby Board," says Mrs. Edinger, "and anyone who talks out of turn will have their name put here. Only babies talk when they're supposed to be quiet!"

When I enter the public school, I am without assistance. Without "low vision" specialists or special education standards, I am without the benefits of proper orientation and mobility training. There are no braille lessons for me, no large print materials. The air flashes like quartz, and I see nothing of the arithmetic lesson. My fingers slide in all directions. I clasp and unclasp the lid of my pencil box, trace the scars on my desk. I pull at my eyelids in an effort to refine the mist.

I must ask a question, some nearly useless thing like how many dogs are on the blackboard. I turn to Janet, who sits next to me, and whisper, "How many dogs are there?"

"I see Stephen talking!" cries the teacher, and there is the staccato of chalk in action. "Stephen's name goes on the Baby Board!"

I am swollen shut, catch myself, sit straight in my chair as laughter breaks around me.

Without an assistant I am forced to listen.

I listen like a person telephoning in the dark.

I listen like the ornithologist who unwraps bird bones from tissue paper.

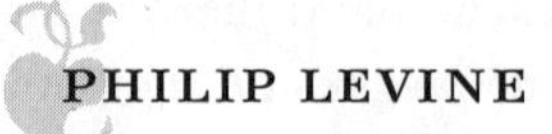

PHILIP LEVINE

from The Bread of Time
Toward an Autobiography

I learned a great deal in my early years. I think this was largely because I loved school, especially on rainy days. When the sky darkened and the rain began to smear the windows, I felt there was no place in the world warmer and friendlier than my fourth-grade classroom at Roosevelt Elementary School. I would look around at the blank faces of my classmates and think how lucky I was to be one of them. My teacher, Mr. Dubrow, was in his first year as a professional, and during the early weeks I could feel his anxiety like a palpable thing. He was the only teacher I ever had who looked up at the clock more than his students; at times he seemed utterly stunned to discover how little it had moved in what must have felt like an eternity. As the year wore on, little by little I could feel him relax and even take a liking to us. I was his favorite because I got a hundred on every exam, even if I had to cheat, and this seemed to confirm his belief in himself as a teacher. He loaned me all sorts of books to read, beginning with the short stories and tales of Nathaniel Hawthorne and concluding with his old history textbooks from college, which were far more enjoyable. At the end of the year, he put one hand on my head, opened his great wet brown eyes as wide as possible, and told me never to stop learning. I promised him I would not.

I'm afraid I broke that promise before I left school. I attended the worst high school in the world. At another high school I might have learned all there was to know about inertia or how bodies in motion tended to stay in motion or why boys and men continued to search for their fathers, but at Wilbur Wright Technical High I learned to keep nothing of value in my locker, to forge my mother's signature, and never to eat in the cafeteria. It was such a sorry place that even the teachers took to playing hooky or showing up late. During my entire senior year my Spanish teacher arrived at our eight o'clock class on time only twice. Usually someone would be posted to watch for her. “Here she comes,” the sentry would shout, and the class would rush to the windows at the back of the room to see her alight from a Yellow Cab, which would then continue down the avenue bearing her boyfriend to whatever life awaited him. We would take our seats, bow our heads to our books, and await her entry. She would arrive slightly breathless with her heavy rabbit coat hanging open and little beads of sweat forming above her upper lip and on her forehead. Always hatless and scarfless, she usually wore a white nylon blouse that plunged enough to reveal her prominent sternum and the tight skin that glowed a rich orange. When she turned to hang her coat on the back of the door, the boys gesticulated wildly, rising out of their seats to shape her rear end, which was certainly neat and tight, or thrust their arms upward in what passed for a symbol of the entry into heaven or the out-and-out charge through the valley of paradise. She always gave us enough time to regain our seats and our composure before turning to greet us. “*Buenos días.*”

AUDRE LORDE

from Zami
A New Spelling of My Name

When I was five years old and still legally blind, I started school in a sight-conservation class in the local public school on 135th Street and Lenox Avenue. On the corner was a blue wooden booth where white women gave away free milk to Black mothers with children. I used to long for some Hearst Free Milk Fund milk, in those cute little bottles with their red and white tops, but my mother never allowed me to have any, because she said it was charity, which was bad and demeaning, and besides the milk was warm and might make me sick.

The school was right across the avenue from the Catholic school where my two older sisters went, and this public school had been used as a threat against them for as long as I could remember. If they didn't behave and get good marks in schoolwork and deportment, they could be "transferred." A "transfer" carried the same dire implications as "deportation" came to imply decades later.

Of course everybody knew that public school kids did nothing but "fight," and you could get "beaten up" every day after school, instead of being marched out of the schoolhouse door in two neat rows like little robots, silent but safe and unattacked, to the corners where the mothers waited.

But the Catholic school had no kindergarten, and certainly not one for blind children.

Despite my nearsightedness, or maybe because of it, I learned to read at the same time I learned to talk, which was only about a year or so before I started school. Perhaps *learn* isn't the right word to use for my beginning to talk, because to this day I don't know if I didn't talk earlier because I didn't know how, or if I didn't talk because I had nothing to say that I would be allowed to say without punishment. Self-preservation starts very early in West Indian families. . . .

. . . by the time I arrived at the sight-conservation kindergarten, braided, scrubbed, and bespectacled, I was able to read large-print books and write my name with a regular pencil. Then came my first rude awakening about school. Ability had nothing to do with expectation.

There were only seven or eight of us little Black children in a big classroom, all with various serious deficiencies of sight. Some of us were cross-eyed, some of us were nearsighted, and one little girl had a patch over one of her eyes.

We were given special short wide notebooks to write in, with very widely spaced lines on yellow paper. They looked like my sister's music notebooks. We were also given thick black crayons to write with. Now you don't grow up fat, Black, nearly blind, and ambidextrous in a West Indian household, particularly my parents' household, and survive without becoming fairly rigid fairly fast. And having been roundly spanked on several occasions for having made that mistake at home, I knew quite well that crayons were not what you wrote with, and music books were definitely not what you wrote in.

I raised my hand. When the teacher asked me what I wanted, I asked for some regular paper to write on and a pencil. That was my undoing. "We don't have any pencils here," I was told.

Our first task was to copy down the first letter of our names in those notebooks with our black crayons. Our teacher went around the room and wrote the required letter into each one of our notebooks. When she came around to me, she printed a large "A" in the upper left corner of the first page of my notebook and handed me the crayon.

"I can't," I said, knowing full well that what you do with black crayons is scribble on the wall and get your backass beaten, or color around the edges of pictures, but not write. To write, you needed a pencil. "I can't!" I said, terrified, and started to cry.

"Imagine that, a big girl like you. Such a shame. I'll have to tell your mother that you won't even try. And such a big girl like you!"

And it was true. Although young, I was the biggest child by far in the whole class, a fact that had not escaped the attention of the little boy who sat behind me and who was already whispering, "Fatty, fatty!" whenever the teacher's back was turned.

“Now just try, dear. I’m sure you can try to print your A. Mother will be so pleased to see that at least you tried.” She patted my stiff braids and turned to the next desk.

Well, of course, she had said the magic words, because I would have walked over rice on my knees to please Mother. I took her nasty old soft smudgy crayon and pretended that it was a nice neat pencil with a fine point, elegantly sharpened that morning outside the bathroom door by my father, with the little penknife that he always carried around in his bathrobe pocket.

I bent my head down close to the desk that smelled like old spittle and rubber erasers, and on that ridiculous yellow paper with those laughably wide spaces I printed my best “AUDRE.” I had never been too good at keeping between straight lines no matter what their width, so it slanted down across the page . . .

A
    U
        D
            R
                E

The notebooks were short and there was no room for anything else on that page. So I turned the page over, and wrote again, earnestly and laboriously, biting my lip,

L
    O
        R
            D
                E

half-showing off, half-eager to please.

By this time, Miss Teacher had returned to the front of the room

“Now, when you’re finished drawing your letter, children,” she said, “just raise your hand high.” And her voice smiled a big smile. It is surprising to me that I can still hear her voice but I can’t see her face, and I don’t know whether she was Black or white. I can remember the way she smelled, but not the color of her hand upon my desk.

Well, when I heard that, my hand flew up in the air, wagging frantically. There was one thing my sisters had warned me about school in great detail: you must never talk in school unless you raise your hand. So I raised my hand, anxious to be recognized. I could imagine what teacher would say to my mother when she came to fetch me home at noon. My mother would know that her warning to me to "be good" had in truth been heeded.

Miss Teacher came down the aisle and stood beside my desk, looking down at my book. All of a sudden the air around her hand beside my notebook grew very still and frightening.

"Well I never!" her voice was sharp. "I thought I told you to draw this letter? You don't even want to try and do as you are told. Now I want you to turn that page over and draw your letter like everyone . . ." and turning to the next page, she saw my second name sprawled down across the page.

There was a moment of icy silence, and I knew I had done something terribly wrong. But this time, I had no idea what it could be that would get her so angry, certainly not being proud of writing my name.

She broke the silence with a wicked edge to her voice. "I see," she said. "I see we have a young lady who does not want to do as she is told. We will have to tell her mother about that." And the rest of the class snickered, as the teacher tore the page out of my notebook.

"Now I am going to give you one more chance," she said, as she printed another fierce A at the head of the new page. "Now you copy the letter exactly the way it is, and the rest of the class will have to wait for you." She placed the crayon squarely back into my fingers.

By this time I had no idea at all what this lady wanted from me, and so I cried and cried for the rest of the morning until my mother came to fetch me home at noon. I cried on the street while we stopped to pick up my sisters, and for most of the way home, until my mother threatened to box my ears for me if I didn't stop embarrassing her on the street.

That afternoon, after Phyllis and Helen were back in school, and I was helping her dust, I told my mother how they had given me crayons to write with and how the teacher didn't want me to write my name. When my father came home that evening, the two of them went into council. It was decided that my mother would speak to the teacher the next morning when she brought me to school, in order to find out what I had done wrong. This decision was passed on to me, ominously, because of course I must have done something wrong to have made Miss Teacher so angry with me.

The next morning at school, the teacher told my mother that she did not think that I was ready yet for kindergarten, because I couldn't follow directions, and I wouldn't do as I was told.

My mother knew very well I could follow directions, because she herself had spent a good deal of effort and arm-power making it very painful for me whenever I did not follow directions. And she also believed that a large part of the function of school was to make me learn how to do what I was told to do. In her private opinion, if this school could not do that, then it was not much of a school and she was going to find a school that could. In other words, my mother had made up her mind that school was where I belonged.

That same morning, she took me off across the street to the Catholic school where she persuaded the nuns to put me into the first grade, since I could read already and write my name on regular paper with a real pencil. If I sat in the first row I could see the blackboard. My mother also told the nuns that unlike my two sisters, who were models of deportment, I was very unruly, and that they should spank me whenever I needed it. Mother Josepha, the principal, agreed, and I started school.

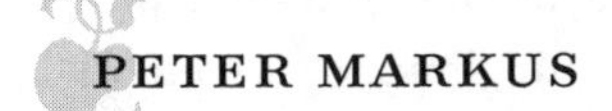

PETER MARKUS

I Am a Cloud

Revisited, or an Open Letter to My Third Grade Teacher

Dear Mrs. Fortner,

I am writing to you now to tell you that I am not a cloud. Remember that day when you told me to imagine that I was a cloud? I couldn't do it. No matter how hard I tried at first, even when I closed my eyes, I couldn't do it. I was just a boy. But you made me write it down, on that piece of paper, those words, *I am a cloud*. And so I did it. I always did as I was told. I was, you will remember, a good student. And when I wrote it down, you told me this: "There, now," you said, "do you see, dear, the paper does not lie. You must be a cloud now." And so I believed what you said. You were, after all, my teacher. I was taught to believe in you. And I became, just like that, like magic, a cloud. I became a floater, a day-dreamer, a *poet*, was what you said I was, in front of the whole class. And the whole class looked at me and laughed. But hey, I was above it all, after all. I was, like the words that I wrote down said I was, a cloud. *I am a cloud floating in the blue sky* was the sentence that I wrote down next. *I can see the tops of trees. I can hear the flapping of the birds' wings. I can touch the sun.* You gave me an A+ for saying what I said. You taped my poem, with a picture that I drew to go along with it, on the classroom wall. You left it there for everyone to see. And you never took it down. Years later, I was told, my poem, "I Am a Cloud," was still Scotch-taped to the cinderblock wall of your room. And like the poem itself, I never came down. I stayed, like a cloud, way up high. I smoked lots of pot. I swallowed whatever pills I could steal out of my sister's purse. It got so that I knew every cloud in the sky by both its first and last name. Mrs. Fortner, teacher of clouds, where are you now? I've been told that you retired from teaching third-graders fifteen years ago. And now my poem is nowhere to be found. I'm guessing that you're probably dead, that maybe you're living dead up in heaven now, and that the clouds below you look to your eyes all the same. Would you recognize me now if you saw me drifting by you? If a cloud floated up to you and told you that it was me, what would you say? Would you believe it? Or would you tell it to stop make-believing, that it's high time to grow up now and come back down to earth? But Mrs. Fortner, I don't want to grow up. I want to be a cloud forever. I want to touch the sun. I want to hear the flapping of birds' wings. Am I crazy for wanting this? I know you're not a head doctor, but if you're alive, please be a teach and tell me what you think.

Forever yours, your student,
Peter Markus

REBECCA McCLANAHAN

Orbit

Miss Ranney's stockings were always straight. I checked the seams each morning as we stood facing the chalkboard, my hand across a place I called a pocket but she called *your heart*, and I pledged allegiance to a flag no bigger than my brother's diaper flapping on the line. We sang of mountains and amber grain, our voices a beat or two behind the warped '45 spinning on the phonograph beside the globe on Miss Ranney's desk. Our world was the *Weekly Reader*, hopscotch, and jump rope, the only war the Cold One which America of course was winning.

Above our heads, a banner of the earth's children: an African boy with corduroy hair, a fur-muffled Eskimo, a golden girl from Holland. I fingered my Brownie badge and renewed my oath to help other people at all times, especially those at home. Oh lucky child, doubly loved, held by the centripetal force of Mother and Miss Ranney. They lived only for my welfare, wrote notes about my progress and pinned them to my shirt, exchanged report card signatures. They knew my height and weight and the date of my polio shots. Each morning Mother locked my thermos and only Miss Ranney could loosen it, leaning over me in her ivory crepe blouse until the cap sighed once, then was free.

Six years later my first stockings were seamed and I thought of Miss Ranney while I sat on the edge of the bathtub shaving the pale brown hairs. It was 1963, before panty hose came to smooth the garter belt's bulge. Later that year, I was in Home Ec tracing my face shape onto a mirror when the intercom crackled the news. School let out early. I came home to my mother watching in black and white. The rest of the orbit swirls out from there: King murdered the week of my senior prom, then Bobby in a hotel just miles from my school while I marched to "Pomp and Circumstance," not knowing that within a year on a July night in the back seat of a Volkswagen bus, I would pledge what was left of my heart to a boy leaving for Vietnam while above us the tired moon finally gave in to a tiny man in gravity boots, planting an American flag.

KENNETH A. McCLANE

The Mitchell Movement

I attended a venerable, brutal, all-boys school in New York City which was—and proudly so—the oldest private school in the United States. When I was a student there, the Collegiate School consisted of a large red historic building—with great porticoes and a Dutch-stepped roof—and a newer, more utilitarian structure.

Collegiate, of course, had its long-held traditions. Most were innocuous; the others—like its penchant to push students to their limits—could be, and far too often were, sinister. Children did learn there; many, however, paid a great price. No one, at least in the twelve years I was matriculated, was not affected: the best students were thick-skinned; another group graduated somewhat punch-drunk; the rest of us departed with something essential missing: we had been violated, but we did not know by what, or how we might get healed. There was just a big gash in our psyches, ineffably dooming us to chase our severed halves, like cut worms.

I constantly remember being the only black in my classes, and the time, on the first day of Spanish class—I was in the fourth grade—when the teacher, Mr. Calvacca, asked me, "Would the colored boy in the red jacket read the sentence?" meaning *me*, the "colored boy," who now was as beet red as his vermilion blazer. Or the time when the music teacher took one of my classmates, who she claimed was making spit balls, and made him stand before the class, fill a six-ounce cup with his own spittle, and drink it down before our terrified eyes. Not only was this act disgusting, but I shall never forget that thin-boned student, trying to create the ghastly meal that he would soon be called upon to swallow.

There are many more such instances—the beating of a boy in the stomach in the Headmaster's office for some minor infraction, the constant dreary verbal bullying—but the result was that never to my knowledge was *any* teacher ever punished for any act of cruelty to his or her charges. The school was a famous one: thousands applied to get accepted; it was the door to Harvard, Heaven, and Respectability; and parents took the school's methods as sacrosanct. Rarely would a parent stick up for his child: my parents scurried to the school when a teacher made a homosexual pass at me in the fifth grade; a famous cartoonist once came to the school to dispel a teacher's notion that his son was "too creative." But these were unusual occasions—as exceptional as finding gold in a neighbor's stream.

Since I was one of the first of two black children in the school's three-hundred-year history, things, of course, grew more complicated. Injustice as I perceived it often flared up Janus-faced. Clearly the place believed certain things, and one could get into trouble for any number of reasons, including laziness, *boyishness*, failure to listen, failure to keep a neat appearance, and so on. But for the black child, in a totally alien environment, everything shimmered with possible associations, imaginings, and repercussions.

In the fourth grade I, of all the students, got myself into an extreme punishment that lasted a year, happening indeterminately but with certainty, for little apparent reason, and with no sense on my part of what I now perceive as its clear intent and clear system. At that time I had a very messy desk, or at least one that my English teacher, Mr. Mitchell, felt was particularly grievous. Mr. Mitchell was a thin, slight man, who walked in a mannered way, as if he thought that the world might steal his spine. In his classes, he could be solicitous one moment, and then quickly turn malevolent, throwing chalk or an eraser at the hapless miscreant. Most of us were scared of him. Indeed, when he gave the homework assignment to name the "Seven Wonders of the Ancient World," I came in the next day with my own list of seven, never realizing that there *actually* were Seven Ancient Wonders—that is, that one could look them up. Instead, I had made up my own tally, including the Great Pyramids, Stonehenge, and some others, happily getting three of the seven right. But when Mr. Mitchell asked for my list, instead of receiving the expected commendation, he grew enraged and yelled at me for five minutes, calling me an "idiot" and "stupid," until he thought I would cry. But I resisted; not that

I didn't want to cry, but because I would not give in. Then, not getting his desired response, Mr. Mitchell continued his diatribe, it seemed for hours. *I will drive him crazy*, I kept repeating to myself, in the way that children, somehow wondrously, invoke the world's irrefutable dictum: that he best survives who refuses to perish.

Finally, thank God, the period was over. But I recall that Mr. Mitchell looked at me wistfully as I left the room, and then, in an apparent change of heart, softly stated, "Please listen better next time."

Indisputably, Mr. Mitchell was unpredictable, and when he first commented on my bedraggled desk, he told me that he wanted it "clean by his next class," which I had the following day. On his request, understandably, I did attempt to bring order to things, putting the papers in a folder, putting the pens, stapler, books, and scissors in their respective places. And on the next day, just at the end of the class's discussion of *Julius Caesar*, Mr. Mitchell inspected my desk and was pleased. "Just keep it neat, McClane," he prompted.

However, the next class, things to Mr. Mitchell's way of thinking had eroded, and two minutes before the class was to end, he ran to my desk, turned the whole thing over, and dumped all its innards over the floor. "Clean it up," he yelled, his face red, angry.

Immediately I began getting my things together so that I would have my desk upright before the beginning of Mr. Rodgers's history class, in ten minutes. And how I tried! But when Mr. Rodgers approached, in his dapper Brooks Brothers grey suit and Princeton tie, I was still trying to gather up all my pens. He looked at me, humorously at first, and then yelled, "McClane, why is your desk such a mess? Look, you're taking up my class time with this foolishness." And then, seemingly moving to the blackboard, he pivoted around, grabbed my desk, and brutally overturned it, sending everything radiating over the floor like slop thrown to pigs. "McClane, you *are* a slob. At the end of class, before lunch, set your things in order."

On the next day I had Mr. Mitchell again, and because I felt certain that my desk was shipshape, when he came to me, again at the end of class, I was anxious but not overly concerned. But then, looking in under the desk's lid, he saw that I had three books resting haphazardly on my papers—clearly not a capital offense, but something I should have known would have been cause for concern. And again, his face turned chameleon-like, from a studied calm to a pall of ready anger, and the desk was upended, its contents—and the telltale books—sent everywhere. "McClane, I am losing patience with you," he simply said and walked out.

Mr. Rodgers, this day, came a touch late so I had been able to get my desk uprighted, although the papers were still a mess, and I had pens sitting like toy soldiers hither and yon. Moving briskly through the class, he went to the board, scribbled a line from George Washington, and began to talk. I felt relieved: this day he would not look at my desk. But then, just after Arthur Soong dazzled us with his superior report on Washington's relationship with the Marquis de Lafayette, Mr. Rodgers paused, seemed to remember something, and then slowly sauntered over to my seat. "Mr. McClane, I *know* your desk is in order. So, let's just see." And upon opening the desk top, this time he threw everything out and then, with great flair, uprooted the desk, telling me, "McClane, this is becoming *my* preoccupation. I am getting very tired of this."

In the upcoming weeks I would suffer variations of the desk inspection and overturning, at various intervals, but always at the end of Mr. Mitchell's class and before Mr. Rodgers's. If it had occurred every day, I might have grown inured to it, but because it happened at irregular intervals I could never anticipate it. And just when I sensed that the teacher's attention had traveled elsewhere, that John Arkin's penchant for idle chatter was now the center of derision and teacherly instruction, Mr. Mitchell would swell into a fury, prance toward me like a terrible eagle, and my desk top would be hauled open, everything within it flung against the floor. And then, of course, in a few short minutes Mr. Rodgers would appear, and my desk, now still in a state of disrepair, would be overturned again.

Later on, I would read about the myth of Sisyphus and learn about every manner of vicious cycle; but in those days I was just a young boy who felt, God knows, that I was at the vortex of an unavoidable process, one in which I would always be ridiculed and harangued. If the teachers were trying to get me to clean my desk, or to teach me the importance of industry and proper purportment (which, I hope, was their larger pursuit), then I guess, at least for them, the ends were justifiable even if the means were cruel. But for me, the whole business suggested that there were things in life that made no sense, that one can get locked in a prison of violence and repeated violence, with no sanctuary for understanding or hope. Clearly, Mr. Mitchell and Mr. Rodgers had connived this scheme to *teach* me something, but in their design that I could never get my desk straight, they made me understand—albeit powerfully and mercilessly—that there are forces in the world that are evil and malevolent, that I had encountered, in Anton Chekhov's wonderful phrase, "Something out of the language of childhood."

My twelve years at the Collegiate School contained episodes where I was called "Nigger" and made to understand in numerous ways that I was inadequate—in schoolwork, my desire to be creative, even in my desire to be *black*. Yet nothing better captures the horror of being young, vulnerable, and menaced than those two teachers—seemingly in lockstep—moving briskly to my desk, seizing its contents (which were, I now realize, pieces of my life— *me*—) and throwing them furiously across the hard, polished floor.

BRENDA MILLER

from "Three Lessons"

I'm crying in the kindergarten classroom, with its fish tank and windowsill garden, with its naptime mats rolled up in the corner and the long chalkboards sifting dust into the air. My mother holds me on her lap, but I know she will have to leave soon, any minute, because it's the first day of kindergarten and mothers aren't allowed to stay; I know this though nothing's been said yet, the rules haven't yet been etched into my brain. Even as I'm crying, I'm taking in every detail of the room—enumerating every toy bucket and truck, every stuffed bear, every baby doll with eyes that close and blink open again. And I take in every detail of my teacher, Mrs. Cordoba, large and florid and magnificent in her muumuu, wafting a scent of lemon and ammonia as she walks among us, talking, but I can't hear a word she says. The other kids have stopped crying by now; I'm the only one left who clutches my mother around the neck, and I know I've crossed the line, but I can't stop, it's out of my control.

And then the student teacher appears (where has she been all this time?), breezing into the room and carrying with her a faint whiff of lilac. She has long brown hair that flips up at her shoulders; it's held back from her freckled face with a tweed headband, and her skirt is pleated in many tiny and perfect rows that open and close like paper fans. She turns to the class—all of us, even me, suddenly hushed, our damp faces upturned to bask in the light of her smile. *I wanna hold your hand, I wanna hold your hand*: the song unfurls from the record player and hovers in the air.

And my hands slip from around my mother's neck. And I wiggle just an inch or two away from her lap, but it could be miles as I feel myself drawn toward this woman, away from what I've always known as home. *Everything will be different now*, I hear a voice echo in my head, as Miss Jenkins turns and looks straight at me, her eyes wide, luring me away from the snug confines of my mother's lap. She wears no Hobo Kelly magic glasses, but she has that same omniscient gaze, the same power to find children and see them, really *see* them. Before I know it, my mother has disappeared and I'm in the hubbub; we're all holding hands and dancing in a circle, a pack of children with one mind—one frantic, beating heart.

An hour later I'm picking out my naptime mat, purple, and unrolling it between Jana and Valentina, girls who will be my friends for years and years to come. There will be many photographs of us as a threesome, with me always in the middle, flanked by these two stalwart girls. I lie down, too excited now to sleep but closing my eyes anyway, because those are the rules, and all around me I feel the bodies of children as they settle down. The giggles subside. The fish tank bubbles. Miss Jenkins and Mrs. Cordoba patrol among us, keeping watch, assuring we'll never come to harm. Together, we'll learn everything we ever need to know.

NAOMI SHIHAB NYE

Last Day of School

The long yellow pencils with promising pointed tips, shrunken to nubs. Trash cans overflow. We've turned in the thick books, though we know there was a lot we skimmed over quickly. Those final chapters, the modern days. We're feeling fond of the grumpy teacher, the smoky chalk groove along the blackboard's rim. Running our fingers along everything we can—nicks in the wooden tops of our desks, snappy rings of a crowded notebook, as we stuff the final papers in, the cool edge of the metal chair. Our many minor mistakes erased the high hopes of far-gone September. We were going to be perfect. We were going to make all As. Today someone who didn't speak to us all year—Freddy? Steve?—speaks suddenly, comfortably, and it is so clear—we could have been friends. We were here all along. The black and white marquee at the edge of the schoolyard says LAST DAY OF SCHOOL JUNE 2. We pin things to that date. A deeper breath, gulp of finer air, extended evenings in the back lot playing "Lost in the Forest," or "Gone from Here." I'm fond of the game called "Families Getting Along." Soft light, peach cobbler, fireflies, a colander of fresh-picked cherries. Our school paintings return to us slightly battered. We smooth their corners. The classroom walls grow emptier by the hour. Someone agrees to take the turtle home.

There are moments we stand back from our classmates and teacher and familiar territory as if trying to contain the details of the scene precisely, in case we need to find our ways here again. CENTRAL SCHOOL, you will remain central in my compass, your red brick certitude, your polished ancient halls. I have marched and circled and bent my head inside you. I have wandered and lost my way. I have been proud, been locked in, been shy, been wounded by a vagrant strip of metal in a doorway, and stitched back together, been punished. In second grade I spoke into the recently-installed intercom, to say my first published poem to the whole school at once and this phenomenon was more exciting than seeing the poem in the magazine. If my lips touched the silver microphone I might be electrocuted. I was never invited to speak into it again though there were many other things I might have said. I pray to Central School as much as I pray to any God or gods. I believe in the tall windows, the rounded porcelain drinking trough. I love eating on a tray. When my parents fight, when my mother locks herself in her bedroom for hours, sobbing, and I press my ear to the door to make sure she is still alive, when my father disappears into the city, I know the school building five blocks from our house has not changed a bit. It would still comfort me if I stepped into it.

It is true I have little interest in the future. When teachers speak of ambition, college, goals, careers, success, my eyes are trailing dust motes in a beam of sun. I want everyone to leave the room so I can go through the trash. Maybe there is something in there I could use right now.

Kindergarten through sixth grade, the school knows us. The school is our stable and we are little horses dashing up the hill to beat the bell every morning. My father is the only Arab father, but he runs for PTA president and is elected. The French Canadian and Italian parents vote for him. He runs for school board later and loses. "I think that was pushing it," says my mother. What does "pushing it" mean? Thinking about the future is pushing it. I would hold us here even when Here hurts, but nothing gives me that power. Only in words on a page can it still be yesterday. Still Walt Whitman, still Abraham Lincoln, Susan B. Anthony, only the words. There were more chapters in that book, I'm sure of it. More tribes and countries we had not discussed.

What I cannot dream then is how I will come back to Central School on the day after the Last Day, forty years later. The custodian pausing in the same front doorway with his wide broom, a dreamy relaxed look on his face. He says, Go right in, it's still there. Look around. Don't tell anyone I haven't emptied the trash cans yet.

I take my time. It's summer, so that's all there is. Because Central School is a historic monument to more people than me, nothing really has changed. Same drinking trough. Same banister and wide stairs. I paw through the trash can in my second grade classroom and claim MY PERSONAL DICTIONARY by ERIC—the "L" page lists "Light, Love, Laugh, Lift, Lose, Little, Loose, Labor." Okay Eric, I say out Loud. A+, man. Everything you'll need for the Life, man, right there on one page. I stick his dictionary in my waistband under my T-shirt, feeling like a pirate, press my forehead against the white bathroom wall tile, down low, where I would have reached in third grade. I did not mean to break John's nose or drive Miss Dreon crazy. I should never *ever* have told Karen to pull down her underpants on the playground. In the gymnasium, the same stage I stood on, could it be, the same burgundy draperies? I shoot a few free throws and make them. I never made them back then. A ring of ghostly girls dances a gypsy dance. Didn't we wear our grandmothers' scarves? And didn't we pledge, pledge, pledge, palms on our chests, every day we lived, pledge to the one nation, the freedom we believed in, didn't we? Fat lot of good.

Forty years later I want to be true to that oddball in a golden gunny-sack dress with purple sleeves. What history taught us, we promised to learn. We would be braver, wiser, than ones who came before. We pledged, and felt proud in the pledging. There would be no more war because the world had seen war; it was terrible and now we knew better things. We would always be rich in our knowing, even if our velvet sacks of quarters gave out, and our mothers' sorrow turned to anger, and our principal went to jail. There were extra red bricks stacked in the corners of our yard, same color as the school. There could still be a project. We would do better this time.

Slow time rapidly passing, watch it, the time we can't believe till a few years after my return to Central School, we're sitting in another auditorium clapping for our own boy crossing a stage on his high school graduation day. He could not find the red tassel for his flat hat, so he is wearing my old black one; he is the only graduate with a black one. Tomorrow I will find the red tassel in the trash, still in the plastic, at home. Care in the details, I always told him. It didn't take. I was a better student than mother, maybe. And now it is too late for new habits. And the headlines count the boys, the men, the women, fallen every day for stupid reasons, cycles of falling, the headlines count and they do not count, and I despise them. Pledging to nothing but what can't be said, to Lost Labor and the Light we smother, for what? We're pushing it.

A thousand miles from the first city, and the parents still fighting in the foyer of my boy's graduation hall, who could believe it? The parents still fighting, like history I guess, old repetitions unresolved, and the books still closing and history's oiled engine clicking and spinning. All over the city of my grown-up years, marquees announcing farewell at every front gate and playground, wishing us well, wishing us a good summer even though you have to look really hard for a firefly now. I blow kisses to every one of them, tears in my eyes and throat and nose. I was a fool, and I will always be a fool and there will never, never, be a last day of school.

GREGORY ORR

from The Blessing

It was in Renssalaerville that I started first grade at the age of five. Though it was 1952, the schoolhouse, like the village itself, was lost in time, a pale-planked, churchish structure perched on a hill at the edge of town. Each morning, the bellrope tugged, the brass bell in its squat tower rang its summons out over the ceaseless stream sound.

There were two teachers in two big rooms—a cluster of desks, a blackboard, and a woodstove in each. One teacher taught first, second, and third grades all in the same room on the ground floor; the other taught fourth, fifth, and sixth on the floor above. After sixth, a bus whisked you up the dirt road out of town, over the hills toward Greenville Central's upper grades twenty miles away.

But here, in each room, a score of us labored, oblivious of any larger world except twice a month when the itinerant art teacher appeared and we all crowded into one room. Balding, with a bland, blank face, it was not his figure, but his outfits that shouted the mysteries of art to our small-town eyes: white shirts and bright string ties, one with a silver bull's skull with a red stone glistening in each eye socket. Each lesson began with his announcement of some seasonal theme like spring or Christmas or a patriotic event—especially the births of notable presidents. Armed with crayons and paper, we'd be off to the races. And as if art was a chaotic contest open to all, our teacher, too, put his gifts and imagination to the task at hand. Half an hour later, each student displayed his or her creation, and lo—the winner (how did one win? who judged?) was given the teacher's drawing as a prize! I remember these odd contests well, having once, with my image of little George attacking the cherry tree with his hatchet, won the teacher's own version of Rembrandt Peale's Washington portrait, the one with puffs of white space at the bottom as if he was standing over a steam grate or peering down from clouds.

On alternate weeks, a music teacher appeared. Again, all six grades duly gathered together. These visiting teachers seemed to me to come from some other world far more sophisticated than I could imagine. Perhaps they weren't traveling teachers at all; perhaps they were only local talent hired for the day—but to me they were as amazing and mysterious as circuit-riding preachers who had the power to dazzle us, their widely scattered and benighted flock, with the gospel of art. Although I firmly believed our drawing teacher was a genius, I was even more in awe of the man who taught us music.

At just the right moment, after announcing the song we would all sing, this mystagogue would produce a round, chrome-silver pitch pipe from his vest pocket and blow a single, clear tone. I assume it was the opening note of the song, but since I was incapable of coming within shouting distance of any designated note, it made no difference. Stunned that this gleaming disk enclosed in its mystic circumference an entire musical scale, I'd stare, dumb and vacant as someone hypnotized by a dangled pocket watch as the rest of the class stumbled its way through the melody.

In those days there was nothing about school I didn't love. But most of all I cherished how simple, predictable, and responsive it was. In school, everything made sense and there were no mysteries, no shadows and silences that stirred vague longings in me. Everything was overt and clear, as if lit by a bright bulb. All my eagerness to please was rewarded there. If I behaved well, I got a pat on the head. Studying hard got me a smile and a scrawled red star on the margin of my paper. I loved it and gave it my heart and soul from the very start. School was the answer to home and to the silences there. . . .

VIVIAN GUSSIN PALEY

from Kwanzaa and Me
A Teacher's Story

Walking through the halls of our school, I have color on my mind. The children who scramble past come in nearly every shade of the birches, pines, and wind-swept dunes of my summers. They are the colors of the chipmunk and trout, the deer and the gull. In point of fact, however, most of the girls and boys are white.

We are a large private school on an urban university campus, an integrated island, both school and neighborhood, within the predominantly black South Side of Chicago. Our school is approximately 65 percent white, 15 percent black, and 10 percent Asian. Perhaps 2 percent of the students are Hispanic and the rest call themselves "other."

Nearly 80 percent of the teachers are white. It is the sort of place the sociology professor does not want for his child. All the colors of woodland and beach do not disguise the attitudes, sounds, and rhythms of our school: it is white. If the professor sat in my classroom, even if he liked my ways with children, he would see the absence of color. More important, perhaps, he would worry about the behavioral monotones of a middle-class white teacher.

"I don't want my baby spending all her time trying to figure out what a white teacher wants her to be," the professor had said. I think I know what he means. As a Jewish child in the Chicago public schools I struggled to fit the mold set by my non-Jewish teachers. . . . I carefully guarded Rosh Hashanah and Yom Kippur along with a few other holidays. The Jewish children stayed home on those days but no teacher ever mentioned the reason for our absence. We understood that we were not to speak of it, that it would sound "too Jewish."

Have the African American children in my classes already learned not to act "too black"? We have books about black children on our shelves and pictures of black heroes on the wall but . . . the professor would say these are not enough. We need more people and curricula that are black. They are right, of course. But I will still be white.

"Call me brown," Kesha had said to me during the first month of school.

"All right," I replied. "And what will you call me?"

"I can call you peach. With spots." She examined my hands. "What are they?"

"Some people call them age spots. I'm getting older."

"What do you call them?" Kesha wondered.

"I guess I don't call them anything. Just spots would be fine."

"Okay, peach with spots for you and brown without spots for me, except this one and this one on my cheek."

Jeremy and Martha are playing "Guess Who?" It is a twenty-question type of game in which one player attempts to identify his opponent's card by eliminating the other possibilities.

"Does your person have a mustache?" asks Jeremy, who is black, of Martha, who is white. "No mustache," Martha responds, and Jeremy places face down on his board all the mustached faces.

"Does your person wear a hat?"

"No hat." Down go the cards with hats.

"Is the person white?" is Jeremy's next question. Martha is puzzled. "What do you mean?" she wants to know. Jeremy repeats his question. "White. Is it white? The person, is he white?"

Martha turns to Annie, who has just arrived. "Jeremy says white. Is it?" she asks, and Annie looks doubtful. The card in question reveals a pink-cheeked, yellow-haired girl, but neither white child knows the girl is called white.

Seventeen of the twenty faces in the game are white, as are eighteen of the twenty-five children in our class, plus two white teachers. Jeremy sits in a sea of white faces yet his question is not understood. I am reminded of the time I said "gentile" in front of my second-grade teacher and she snapped at me, "You mean Christian!" My face was hot with confusion and embarrassment. I had thought Christian was the word we weren't supposed to say.

I call to Kesha, who is coloring at a nearby table. "Come see if there are any white faces in this game, will you?" She stares at me.

"They're all of them white," she answers, walking over to the game. "Except for just this one, and this, and this isn't." Kesha watches Martha with interest. "Aren't you white?" she asks her. "You look white."

"I'm pink," Martha responds. She is six years old, bright as can be, and she doesn't know she belongs to what we call the white race. It wouldn't matter except for the fact that Jeremy and Kesha and Rasheem and Ashley, our four black children, *do* have that information and we all live together in the same classroom. Later, when I describe the scene to Jeremy's father, he thinks it's funny. "I'm not surprised," he says. "White kids don't have to know that."

Nor white teachers, it seems. When I introduce my Magpie characters, I specifically refer to the brown skin and African origins of Princess Annabella, Prince Kareem, and Kwanzaa. I do not feel I must explain that everyone else is white. Princess Alexandra, the king and queen, Corporal Thomas and his son Raymond, and all the others apparently do not require racial identities. They simply *are*.

However, now the secret is out and I'll have to talk about it. After the game, I call everyone to the rug next to the piano where most of our discussions are held, and I bring the black and white dolls with me.

"Annabella is black," I begin, holding up each doll in turn, "and Alexandra is white. If Princess Annabella lived in America she would also be called African American. Or brown. Kesha calls herself brown. And Mrs. Barnes sometimes says she is a person of color. Now, Martha calls herself pink and Kesha once said I was peach with spots. Jeremy's mom calls us Caucasian. And Maria's dad says 'Anglo.' But most people would call me, Martha, Princess Alexandra, and a whole lot of people in this room white." Why am I doing this in such a clumsy way? It would have been better simply to describe the Guess Who? incident and let the children involved explain what happened, as I usually handle such events. Obviously the subject is an awkward one for me.

"What color is Magpie?" Rasheem asks.

Bless you, my child. Magpie to the rescue. Again. "He's black and white, with a bit of shiny green and blue showing when he spreads his tail." Everyone looks up at the colorful display of children's drawings on the wall, of magpies, brown and white princesses, and red-headed Raymonds. The orange flower people are there from a past series of stories and so is Kwanzaa, the newest member of the picture gallery. He is darkest of all, sitting in a boat, getting ready for the trip home to Africa.

"I'm not a color," says Vijay, who is from India. Jeremy leans over to ask, "Would you like to be light brown?" Vijay nods, satisfied.

MAJ RAGAIN

Under the Guidance of Falling Petals

Polio burned its way through me in August of 1949, just as I was ready to start the fourth grade at Central School, Olney, Illinois. Poliomyelitis. Infantile paralysis. The fear of every parent. Lethargy, thirst, fever. A spinal tap confirmed bulbar polio, the mean strain of virus, the worm that ate the apple. A year in hospitals, therapy, then home. Full length metal leg braces. A corset back brace. High back wooden wheelchair. I was nine years old, a slight, pale boy with a head full of blue sky and muddy river, an arrow frozen in mid-flight.

Illinois state law stipulated that my education be continued. Education, from the Latin *educare*, to be led forth, that I might enter society as a responsible and productive citizen and find my place in history. The Richland county school board deemed that I be visited by a teacher for two hours each weekday afternoon. I didn't want to be visited by anyone. I couldn't meet people's eyes the first time they saw me. I was safe in my room, dreaming, listening to the radio, riding the airwaves on my bed, that small boat, whispering adventures to myself. Most days, I thought of myself as a pirate, the first stirrings of a secret life, a kind of movie screen inside my head. A buccaneer. A swashbuckler. I came across that word and I loved to whisper it, a threat, a promise. Swashbuckler, swashbuckler. A man of action who could buckle your swash if you weren't careful, who lived by his own laws and took what he wanted. I flew the skull and crossbones. My country 'tis of thee I sing. My beard was blue. My heart was black. I didn't want any visitors to my hideaway where I sat alone amidst the plunder, my cutlass stashed beneath my bed.

That first school day in September, I waited for the teacher to arrive. I couldn't figure out how to present myself, where to sit, how to meet her eyes, what to say. To this day that plagues me. Finally, I decided to take off my braces and sit on the bed, to lean against the wall for support, my skinny legs tucked Indian fashion, just a regular fella at ease with himself and the world. I practiced what to say. *Oh, hello,* in an offhand way, not giving away much but acting both pleased and surprised to see her. I'd seen adults pull this off. I heard her car in the gravel driveway. I peeked out from behind the curtain. The car was light blue, shiny, maybe new, nothing like that in this lakeside neighborhood of patched up summer cottages. What if she was a rich lady who would scoff at our poverty? I flushed as Mom greeted her kindly at the front door and brought her to my room where I sat like a bump on a log. *Major, this is Miss Effie Eberhardt. She is going to be your teacher. Oh, hello,* I muttered, my gaze reading the floor.

Effie was maybe forty, prematurely gray, unmarried, a woman of independent resolve who belonged to herself and no other. She was, as Mom put it, "fixity"—that is, one who spent time and care fixing herself up (not down), love's red rose lipstick, hair carefully spray-shaped, bejeweled eyeglasses she sometimes wore around her neck on a silver chain, the tasteful blush of rouge. She never wore a house dress, rather one of those movie star Loretta Young full-skirted pleated bells that crinkled and tolled as she sat down on the edge of my bed to begin the day's instruction. I had never met anyone like her. She loved the pages of books and tasted words as if they were food that sustained her life, the alphabet soup, the ink broth.

It was through Effie Eberhardt that poetry found me. Onc day, she read aloud a poem by Vachel Lindsay, who was born and raised in Springfield, Illinois, two or three hours north of Olney. It was titled "The Leaden-Eyed."

> Let not young souls be smothered out
> before they do quaint deeds and fully flaunt their pride.
> It is the world's one great crime

its babes grow dull, its poor
are limp, ox-like and leaden-eyed.

Not that they starve, but starve so dreamlessly.
Not that they sow, but seldom reap.
Not that they serve, but have no gods to serve.
Not that they die, but that they die like sheep.

A shiver of recognition ran through me. I didn't hear this in the talk around me, the little talk that diminishes us and tethers us to the world of things. The voice in this poem, not Effie but Lindsay, was calling me out, challenging me not to starve dreamlessly, to awaken and stay awake. I felt its truth in my breastbone. And Lindsay had found a way for the poem to hold the meaning, as a hive holds honey. I have returned to this poem till I know it by heart. I say it aloud at odd moments, at a stoplight or looking out a midnight window, as a way of summoning courage, remembering what I must do, to dream, to serve, to sow. Of course, I didn't think in these terms at eleven or so, but when I read that poem now, more than fifty years later, I can still hear what I heard then. I can dip my tin cup in that clear, shining water—different water, same river—my first sense that there is something imperishable and boundless in what we do, saved inside words.

In time, I became stronger on my crutches, spent less time in the chair. I'd walk laps around the little circle driveway by the house, thrusting myself forward with my arms. Then, the doctor at the clinic broke the news to Mom and Dad: scoliosis, curvature of the spine. It was happening quickly, my spine bending into an s-shape, the muscles around it too weak to provide support. The answer, said the man in the white coat, was the Milwaukee back brace, a new medical prosthesis. I remember how cold the word sounded—prosthesis—nothing I would whisper in the night. So, they fitted me with a steel cage, vertical bars every six inches or so from hip to head, a steel halo around my brow, with a leather chin cup which immobilized my head, a strap across my forehead and a steel tightening screw in the back, with a quarter-sized hex nut protruding. *He'll have to wear this till the spine straightens*. That was the sentence handed down. I returned home, back in the wheelchair. I had to be moved about like a giant vase, placed here and there.

When it was time for Effie to resume her visits, I positioned myself on my bed against the woodwork, steadying myself with the screw head against the wood. When Effie came into the room and saw me, she burst into tears at the sight of the boy in the iron mask, the erector set Humpty Dumpty, the prisoner of Zenda. She sat on the couch with Mom and composed herself before she came back into my room and sat down. I felt her sadness to be greater than mine and couldn't understand why. Every weekday I sat there for a couple of hours up against the wall, listening, learning: Orion, lepidoptera, Pocohontas, Mohican, Northwest Territory, Eric the Red, John Wilkes Booth, Madagascar, the Andes, Ponce de León, Rio De Janeiro, Nagasaki, Hiroshima, turquoise, triceratops. The words extended outward, a bridge to the world. I wrote them down in a big yellow tablet; some were stones, which, when cut and polished, glinted like gems: Dakota, lizard, oxen, pistol. Each word knew what it meant long before I read it.

This summer, fifty years later, when I returned to the cottage, to the same room where I sleep when I visit, I traced with my fingertips the woodwork scarred by the steel hex stud on the back of the Milwaukee brace. The scar, a pattern of gouges about the size of my hand, is still visible: a glyph, a character, a tattoo, an etching from a prisoner scratching the days on the cell wall. It marked my hitching post. It marked my time in the stocks. It was one of my first attempts to make my mark on the world, my markings on the page. When I graduated from the eighth grade and my home-schooling came to an end, Effie presented me with a gift, a pencil sharpener, a Boston model RS. Dad bolted it to a wooden base. Crank and sharpen. Bring it to a point. Mark. Sharpen again. It is still with me. I have marked these pages with pencils sharpened on it. I close my eyes. My fingertips trace these lines, the welt of the words, the gouges in the paper, that woodwork.

Effie did eventually marry, a kindly fellow named Bob Ulm, a prosperous local farmer. Dad, Mom, and I drove out to see her. I was leaving for college in Terre Haute. It was autumn. The farmhouse was surrounded by apple trees, the smell of vinegar sugar in the air, the heavy golden light shafting through the boughs. She was working in the yard, put down her rake and walked over to the car to greet us. I wanted to tell her of my resolve not to starve dreamlessly, and that, as she stood there, I knew a great wind was carrying us all across the sky. I didn't say much. A handful of words. A grocery bag of apples. A brush of her lips on my cheek. A last wave as we turned down the driveway. She died a year later, cancer. I can still hear her voice in my head.

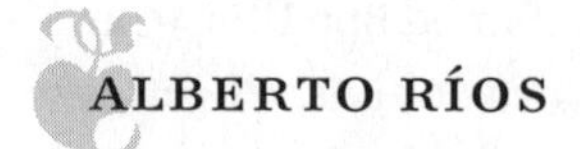

ALBERTO RÍOS

from "The Body of My Work"

> What the United States does best is to understand itself. What it does worst is understand others.
> —*Carlos Fuentes*

I've said many times that my first language was more or less Spanish. It's true but it's not true, too. Mine was Spanish the way potlucks are meals, which is an apt comparison, I think. My language, finally, consisted of whatever words would get me dinner. In that sense, my first language was the same as everybody's. And in this moment, pointing at my mouth was as strong as anything I could say, as strong as "*dame comida*" or "give me food."

It was a child's existence, and children find their way. Pointing and winking and laughing are part of the vocabulary mix. Then first grade happens. First grade is a name for that time when adults start to tell children how to find their way, rather than simply letting them, and there's confusion. First grade is often quite abruptly another kind of meeting place, another kind of food and language.

My friends also spoke Spanish, and some English and some pointing and some Yaqui and some border and some Papago. We spoke it—this *it* we had created—easily and all the time, framing ourselves in this carnival language made of linguistic high-wire acts and rhetorical elephants, fluent tigers and eloquent cannonballs. We were all *bukis* getting around on our *patamobiles,* always asking for *chicle* to chew and Fanta to drink. Our parents drove around in *troques*, or caught *el bus*. We spoke this language easily until we got into the first grade classroom, where on the very first day our teacher said, "You can't speak Spanish in here." Whatever I was speaking, whatever we were all speaking, it must have had enough Spanish in it to make it Spanish altogether, at least in the school's sensibility.

You can't speak Spanish in here. We all looked around at each other, raising our hands politely. We tried to tell the teacher that we could, of course we could. We could speak Spanish anytime, and other things too. Couldn't she hear? This was good, we thought, because it was something we could do, something we could show her. We all laughed.

But no, she said, she meant we were *not* to speak Spanish, that if we did she was going to swat us.

And that was bad. Not only that, but anyone who did speak it and couldn't speak any English at all would have to go to "1-C." That was the name of the grade for kids who couldn't manage in all English, and 1-C didn't count for a grade because if you went there you still had to come to first grade the next year. First grade again. It was like failing. It's like whatever you did in there didn't count. Even as first graders we understood that much, even if we couldn't articulate it. 1-C was like flunking before you even began.

And it was Spanish you spoke in there. The message about Spanish was clear, and if the threat of 1-C weren't enough, we were told we would be swatted even if we spoke Spanish on the playground, just like for saying a "dirty" word. I don't know if 1-C was something that happened across the country in the 1950s or if it was just the Southwest, but it was an effective tactic. We knew that anybody who went there never caught up. And, just like never catching up in any of the playground games, it meant *you lose.*

> After all, when you come right down to it,
> how many people speak the same language
> even when they speak the same language?
> —*Russell Hoban*

I think people's hearts were in the right place in trying to get us to speak English in preparation for the adult world and the place in which we lived, and I don't sense any huge, evil plan at work. But that's almost worse.

We got our rewards for speaking English, though, and they were clear: for lack of a better word, we got the wonderful first grade *stuff*! Desks, pencils, cubbyholes, clay, chalkboards, paints, butcher paper, maps. Well, we didn't actually know about maps, yet, but we liked the string that hung from them in front of the chalkboard—we could tell this was for pulling. This was all real stuff, stuff we didn't have at home. Not even close.

Stuff! We wanted it! It was our job to want it—we were first graders, after all. And if it took learning English, we weren't stupid—we could do that. Two weeks tops. We could, and we did. And well, maybe too well.

The thing is, we didn't stop learning. That's the part nobody talks about very well.

A bargain was being struck, one that you couldn't go home and talk to your parents about. If Spanish was something you were hit for, and you get hit for doing something bad, Spanish then must be bad. That wasn't hard to figure out. We didn't articulate it; we just felt it. We knew what getting swatted would feel like.

Speaking English, on the other hand, got you *stuff*.

> The genius of democracies is seen not only in
> the great number of new words introduced
> but even more in the new ideas they express.
> —*Alexis de Tocqueville*

In second grade the equation widened its orbit. If Spanish was bad, and our parents spoke Spanish, they then must be bad people. In that way, in that almost scientific and mathematical way, we learned to be ashamed of them. What two and two adds up to, after all, is exactly what we were learning. But it was far more than numbers. We suddenly were put into the position of having to take care of our parents, because they didn't seem to get it. They didn't seem to understand it as well as we did. They acted as if nothing was wrong.

So, how do you take care of your parents at school? The clear answer for us was: Don't let them come to school. Don't let them show up. The teacher tried to convince us otherwise, and would give us PTA meeting notices, which were in English. She'd say,

"Take this home to your parents." As if we were dumb enough to fall for that one.

We'd say, "Yes, ma'am" and put the notices in our notebooks. But on the way to the school bus, we'd do our walks, and as part of our walks we'd calmly drop the notes into the garbage can at the end of the playground. It was our little ritual, and we were true to it. We didn't talk about it.

The garbage can, by the way, had an interesting word written on it. The word was *basura*. It didn't say "trash," which is what the word meant in English, because when you want people to do something, you use whatever language it takes. So we got the PTA notices in English, but "trash" in Spanish.

We threw our notes away because we loved our parents, and that was the only way we could take care of them. I knew that if I took the notes home, because my parents were parents, they'd respond. I knew that because they were *my* parents, they'd come to school if they were asked. And I knew that if my father opened his mouth at school, Spanish might come out. And if Spanish came out, well, that was it for him; he'd have to get in the swat line.

I laugh now at the thought of my parents getting swatted because that is so clearly second-grade reasoning. But we *were* second graders, and it's the only kind of reasoning we had.

SUZANNE RIVECCA

The Music Teachers of St. Augustine's Elementary

None of them last long. The first one is large and imposing, wearing blue shirt-dresses that swing just above her nylon calves. Her hair is iron-gray and swept into a stiff marcelled helmet, and her glasses have silver chains. On the first day she marches in, faces us, and sings out stridently: "Hel-lo boys and girls!"

We stare at her. She continues to sing.

"Re-peat after me!" Her singing is completely joyless, militaristic, her voice full-bodied but corroded with rust, like the iron hull of a great ship. "Repeat!" she sings. "Hel-lo, boys and girls!"

Lamely, we half-murmur, half-sing, "Hello boys and girls."

"No!" she roars. She is still singing. "I'm not a boy! I'm not a girl! I am Mrs. Stykos!"

We stare.

"I say 'hel-lo, boys and girls'; you say, 'hel-lo Mrs. Stykos!' One more time we'll try a-gain!"

She will not stop singing. Throughout her brief tenure, she sings every word. We are supposed to do the same. When we forget and speak normally—"Can I go to the bathroom?"—she makes us sing it to her, with that ramrod, stiff-spined Hitler-Youth enunciation, until she is satisfied. She yells and screams, veins bulging like exposed wires in her shiny forehead, but always in song. She makes some of us cry. It is disconcerting to be reprimanded in the key of F; it is like a musical, like *Annie Get Your Gun* gone horribly wrong and turned on you in wrath.

One day she does not come. There is no explanation. In her place is a young woman with Candies sneakers, stringy Suzanne Vega hair, and plastic-framed glasses. She has not only composed her own song, but has choreographed a bizarre dance to complement it. We learn that she expects us to shamble aimlessly around the classroom, twiddling our wrists *cucaracha*-style, while singing

The Virgin Mary had a baby boy
The Virgin Mary had a baby boy
The Virgin Mary had a baby boy
And she said that His name was—
HUH!!!—
Je-SUS!

At the climax of the stanza—that grunting, vaguely lustful, crudely declarative *HUH!!!*—we are instructed to freeze in place and stamp one foot down hard. Then let the name of Jesus burst from our lips, a big post-boom like the aftershock of an earthquake, give it a second to sink in, and start all over from the beginning.

We perform this song at the Christmas recital, throwing ourselves into it with half-mocking abandon, making the *HUH* as basely suggestive and lascivious as possible, rolling our little wrists like flamenco dancers and bringing our feet down hard on the stage, a big collective thump for Jesus that leaves the teacher beaming with pride, the principal puzzled, and the parents aghast. The Candies lady does not return after Christmas break.

Instead there is a man. He is the only male we have ever seen sing anything besides hymns, in front of us, on purpose. He has a black mustache and he conducts us as we go through the scales, his eyes closed, his narrow face twisted as if in pain or ecstasy. He plays classical music on a record player and closes his eyes.

There are rumors among us:

He is gay.

He is a child molester.

He is the long-lost son of Mrs. Stykos, or the long-lost lover of the Candies lady.

Mr. Swinzick doesn't last either, because we drive him out. He doesn't do anything wrong. He just fails to convince us of his authority. Mrs. Stykos and the Candies lady were hated, but accepted as the natural doyennes—tyrannical and cartoonish, flaky but eminently self-assured—of scales and dances and dippy songs. That was their province. Mr. Swinzick, on the other hand, does not belong among us. He was not made to corral and bully us into musical literacy via *John Jacob Jingleheimer Schmidt*. And so he is rejected, instinctively expelled from our sullen presence like a pathogen swarmed and flushed out by antibodies. Before we know it, we have mocked and taunted and ignored him into sheer insensibility, and he quits. Some of us feel bad. Some of us don't. Then comes the next one, a blond lady in a striped turtleneck sweater. She smells like unwashed hair, and her favorite thing is to make us sing Kumbaya while waving our hands above our heads—

"Reach for the sky, kids—oh, Lor-ord, Kumbaya"—and, like twenty warring conductors' batons, day after day, our small arms all go up.

LUIS J. RODRIGUEZ

from Always Running
La Vida Loca, Gang Days in L.A.

We didn't call ourselves gangs. We called ourselves clubs or *clicas*. In the back lot of the local elementary school . . . five of us gathered in the grass and created a club—"Thee Impersonations," the "Thee" being an Old English usage that other clubs would adopt because it made everything sound classier, nobler, *badder*. It was something to belong to—something that was ours. We weren't in boy scouts, in sports teams or camping groups. Thee Impersonations is how we wove something out of the threads of nothing.

"We all taking a pledge," Miguel Robles said. "A pledge to be for each other. To stand up for the *clica*. Thee Impersonations will never let you down. Don't ever let Thee Impersonations down."

Miguel was eleven years old like the rest of us. Dark, curly-haired, and good-looking, he was also sharp in running, baseball, and schoolwork—and a leader. Miguel was not prone to loudness or needless talking, but we knew he was the best among us. We made him president of our club.

Thee Impersonations was born of necessity. It started one day at the school during lunch break. A few of us guys were standing around talking to some girls—girls we were beginning to see as women. They had makeup and short skirts. They had teased hair and menstruations. They grew breasts. They were no longer Yolanda, Guadalupe, or María—they were Yoli, Lupe, and Mari.

Some of the boys were still in grass-stained jeans with knee patches and had only begun getting uncontrollable hard-ons. The girls flowered over the summer, and it looked near impossible for some of us to catch up.

Older dudes from junior high school, or even some who didn't go to school, would come to the school and give us chilled looks as they scoped out the young women.

That day, a caravan of low-scraping cars slow-dragged in front of the school. A crew of mean-looking *vatos* piled out, armed with chains, bats, metal pipes, and zip guns.

"Thee Mystics rule," one of them yelled from the other side of the school fence.

Thee Mystics were a tough and up-and-coming group. They fired their rigged .22s at the school and broke a couple of windows with stones. They rammed through the gate and front entrances. Several not-so-swift dudes who stood in their way got beat. Even teachers ran for cover. Terror filled everyone's eyes.

I froze as the head-stomping came dangerously my way. But I was also intrigued. I wanted this power. I wanted to be able to bring a whole school to its knees and even make teachers squirm. All my school life until then had been poised against me: telling me what to be, what to say, how to say it. I was a broken boy, shy and fearful. I wanted what Thee Mystics had; I wanted the power to hurt somebody.

Police sirens broke the spell. Dudes scattered in all directions. But Thee Mystics had done their damage. They had left their mark on the school—and on me.

RICHARD RODRIGUEZ

from "Asians"

The U.S. Army took your darling boy, didn't they? With all his allergies and his moles and his favorite flavors. And when they gave him back, the crystals of his eyes had cracked. You weren't sure if this was the right baby. The only other institution as unsentimental and as subversive of American individuality has been the classroom.

In the nineteenth century, even as the American city was building, Samuel Clemens romanced the nation with a celebration of the wildness of the American river, the eternal rejection of school and shoes. But in the red brick cities, and on streets without trees, the river became an idea, a learned idea, a shared idea, a civilizing idea, taking all to itself. Women, usually women, stood in front of rooms crowded with the children of immigrants, teaching those children a common language. For language is not just another classroom skill, as today's bilingualists would have it. Language is *the* lesson of grammar school. And from the schoolmarm's achievement came the possibility of a shared history and a shared future. To my mind, this achievement of the nineteenth-century classroom was an honorable one, comparable to the opening of the plains, the building of bridges. Grammar-school teachers forged a nation.

A century later, my own teachers encouraged me to read *Huckleberry Finn*. I tried several times. My attempts were frustrated by the dialect voices. (*You don't know about me without you have read* . . .) There was, too, a confidence in Huck I shied away from and didn't like and wouldn't trust. The confidence was America.

Eventually, but this was many years after, I was able to read in Huck's dilemma—how he chafed so in autumn—a version of my own fear of the classroom: Huck as the archetypal bilingual child. And, later still, I discerned in Huck a version of the life of our nation.

DAVID ROMTVEDT

from "Some Shelter"

There is a song I was taught in school during the 1950s titled "Duck and Cover." It was supposed to help us remember what to do in the event of a nuclear attack. More importantly, it was supposed to convince us that there could be a safe place in a world at war. The atomic bomb would fall and we would duck and cover and it would be OK. There wasn't a child in the room who didn't know this was a baldfaced lie, the height of adult mendacity—as the older boys said, "Bullshit."

During recess, we sat in the dirt by a chain-link fence at the far edge of the school grounds and talked about what would really happen when the bomb fell. The consensus was we would all be dead. For some of us it would be immediate. For others it would be slower and, we feared, more agonizing. These would get to live a little while before their skin fell off and their hair fell out and they died. (We didn't know yet about cancer twenty and thirty years down the line.)

In my seventh-grade science class we had to crawl under our desks during bomb drills. The teacher made the girls pull their skirts over their heads for protection. We boys saw the girls' underwear and wondered how pulling their skirts over their heads would help the girls survive the atomic bomb. Someone complained, and one day the science teacher was no longer among us. Later I learned that even a single layer of fabric could shield one's skin from the first blast effects of the bomb. In Japan, bomb victims were terribly burned except where their clothing had covered their skin.

The anthropologist Margaret Mead believed the entire world could be divided into two categories of people: those born before the atomic bombs were dropped on Hiroshima and Nagasaki, and those born after. If you were born before, you believed that life would go on. No matter how hard things got, no matter what depths of poverty or deprivation you experienced, life would go on. The sun and the moon, the deep blue sky, the birds that sang outside your window not caring if you noticed—it would all go on.

Those born after the bomb do not suffer this delusion. We know there is no safe place in this world we have made.

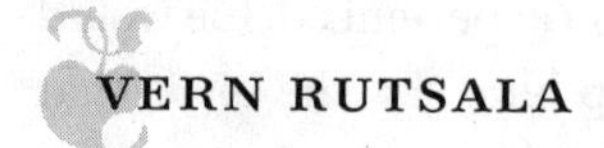

VERN RUTSALA

Some of Us

Remember how they made us sit with our hands folded, how whispering was a crime and passing notes so dangerous only the bravest or most foolhardy dared try it. They were testing us, we knew, hoping our spirits would break like the teacher's chalk. They said day-dreaming was against the law, but some of us escaped, slipping out windows and over cyclone fences, some of us flying away with heads like balloons. We taught our dogs to love the flavor of homework and became expert forgers of our parents' signatures. We knew they were teaching us how to die but some of us said no in our stealthy and stubborn ways.

SCOTT RUSSELL SANDERS

The Real Questions

As I raced through high school, chasing ideas and basketballs and girls, everybody who knew me felt certain that I would study mathematics and science in college, most likely physics, because I was obsessed with uncovering the secrets of the universe. The school principal, the guidance counselor, my teachers, the minister at church, the commander at the arsenal, my parents, and my friends, all agreed that I was destined to become a scientist. How could I think otherwise?

My sure future was complicated one day when the flamboyant young instructor who taught my senior courses in English and French, Eugene Fahnert, called me aside to ask if I had thought what else I might study in college apart from science. Not really, I confessed.

"You don't want your mind to become narrow, do you?" he asked.

"No, sir."

"Then make sure you sign up for some humanities courses every semester. Good solid ones you can get your teeth into. Literature, history, philosophy, art. That way, when you become a scientist, you'll know things that science can never teach you. And you'll hold on to the questions that science can't answer."

"Sounds like a good idea," I said.

"Would I have suggested a bad idea?" said Mr. Fahnert. "Just remember, don't ever give up your questions. Treasure them. Live them. Follow wherever they lead."

At the time I had not read Rilke, who gave the same advice to an aspiring poet in a famous little book, so I heard this call to cherish my questions coming from Mr. Fahnert alone, and that was authority enough. Of all my teachers in high school, he was the one who took the greatest joy in using his mind. He made learning seem as natural as breathing. It helped that he was young, still in his twenties, that he had served in the Army, had lived in

Germany, had climbed mountains, that he skied and cooked and sang, and that he loved books. He was tall, athletic, wavy-haired, with a defiant nose almost as big as my own, and he spoke English in a refined way that made it sound like an exotic language. While directing our school plays during the most fearful months of the Cold War, he would comment as freely on A-bombs or spies as he would on our acting. He convinced me that everything we do matters, that every hour can be charged with meaning, no matter how risky or bleak the world might seem.

Because of Mr. Fahnert, during that last year of high school I wrote down the questions that I used to lie awake wondering about. Here's the list:

How did the universe come to be?

What can we know of the power that sets everything moving?

How did life emerge from matter?

How did consciousness arise from life?

What is the role of mind in the universe?

How should we live?

What are the grounds for that "should"?

Why is there suffering?

Why are humans destructive and cruel?

Does anything of the self survive death?

What is our place in nature?

Do we have a purpose?

Do *I* have a purpose?

What is my true self?

I've held on stubbornly to those questions ever since—or perhaps they've held on to me. Although I don't expect to find conclusive answers, the search has taught me much of what I know.

SUSAN RICHARDS SHREVE

from Tales Out of School
Contemporary Writers on Their Student Years

The first day of first grade and I'm sitting in the front row, chewing off the collar of the dress my mother made me, a habit I had of eating the cotton collars of several outfits a year—a condition of general agitation that would be corrected today with regular doses of Ritalin. I'm watching Mrs. Comstock, soft, plump, weary, and very old, write on the blackboard.

"Who reads?" she asks.

I put up my hand. I don't read and wonder as I look around the room whether the other students with their hands up are telling the truth.

"Good," Mrs. Comstock says, satisfied that we're off to a fine start. "I'm going to write down the rules for First Grade, Section A, Mrs. Comstock's class."

1. NO lateness
2. NO impudence
3. NO speaking out in class
4. NO whispering
5. NO bathroom visits during class
6. NO morning recess unless classwork is completed
7. NO food in the classroom
8. NO temper tantrums
9. NO pushing or shoving when you line up
10. NO tears

I'm extremely pleased as I watch the list run down the blackboard. Although I can't read, do not even want to learn if it means, as I'm afraid it will, giving up the hours sitting next to my mother or father in my small bed while they read to me—I do recognize the word *NO*. I even count the number of *NO*s filling up the blackboard. There are ten.

"So," Mrs. Comstock says, turning around to face us. "Who can read me the rules?"

I don't raise my hand but there I am sitting directly in front of her and without a second's hesitation, she calls my name. I don't even stop to think.

"No, no, no, no, no, no, no, no, no, no," I say without taking a breath.

THEODORE R. SIZER

from The Red Pencil
Convictions from Experience in Education

I was fourteen and a tenth grader in high school when I first tackled "second-year" Latin. Our instructor was our school's most celebrated scholar-teacher, Joseph Barrell. Behind his back, we called him "Joe." To his face, it was "Sir" or "Mister Barrell," titles expected in a traditional school in 1946.

I had experienced "first-year" Latin in various gentle forms in my elementary school and during my initial year at the Pomfret School, the then-all-male boarding school in northeastern Connecticut where I was to confront Joe Barrell. Throughout, I had struggled. Latin, especially Latin grammar, was for me terra incognita, in spite of the persistent ministrations of warm-hearted Classics teachers in seventh, eighth, and ninth grades. I knew that Joe would be a challenge for me. I devoutly hoped that I would not be a challenge for him.

Insensitively, perhaps, the dozen or so of us in our class never recognized much warmth in Joe's heart. He was to our eyes an "old" teacher (when, in fact, he was a Yale graduate student in English finishing his Ph.D. thesis on Percy Bysshe Shelley and his circle). The "oldness" arose from his formality and formidable intellect. His teacher's desk was on a low platform backed against a chalkboard, facing several high windows. He looked down at us. Before him were rows of bolted-down flip-top wooden desks, most of them festooned with small carvings clandestinely engraved by long past predecessor Latin and Greek students. Fading prints of ancient poets and historians furbished the walls.

We started with Caesar (or was it Cornelius Nepos?). Barrell set a prescribed number of lines each night. In class the next day he would randomly pick some boy to start off with the translation of the first assigned sentence. If that unlucky leadoff batter came close to providing an accurate rendition, Joe moved in order along that student's row demanding that the next sentence be translated. If, on the other hand, the first boy had struck out, or clearly had done little of the homework, the second boy had to tackle the sentence that the first had bollixed. This being the daily routine, once Joe had signaled which boy in which row was to open the translation, we all had a fair idea of just when our time to perform would come. We could not easily identify the precise sentence that we would have to confront, as we never surely knew who might flub and have his sentence passed along. We calculated nonetheless, making quick judgments of the likelihood that each particular student would or would not deliver to Joe's satisfaction. We waited, clammy with anticipation, for the moment of our judgment.

What really riveted our attention, however, was Joe's grade book, or, more accurately, the pencil he used to inscribe his judgment of our performances in a small, bound ledger. Barrell would say, "Barnes, translate," listen carefully, and then record a grade. We became experts (we believed) in tracking the movement of his pencil. A. Or B-. Or—please, please make it not be so!—E. By the end of the class we all, save the few Classics Hot Shots, were ready to explode with tension.

That pencil and its penalties remain with me as a painful token of my battle both with Latin and with the notion that my struggles could be so neatly reduced to a cold expression, say a D, in Joseph Barrell's little book. Class with Joe was a place to show off in one prescribed way what we had done on our own. We all were held to precisely the same narrow standard (*agricolam* is in the accusative case or it isn't), and the daily test was the translation of Latin into coherent English. Joe did give some brief lectures on the context of the texts, but the action that counted was all in precise decoding. And so that pencil became my torturer. It was unrelenting in its impersonality.

Many years later my wife, Nancy, pinned a small drawing and a bit of poetry over the desk at which she spent endless weekends grading high school history papers, a winsome piece she had discovered in the *New York Times*. The cartoon depicts a gnome-ish man with a long, pointed nose. The title is "The Red Pen." The text is by R. F. Pease: "It slides swiftly across paper, brushing errors off the page—it strikes terror into punctuation. Red ink acts with accuracy, finding fault, doing its job." Joseph Barrell insisted on accuracy, finding fault when error reared its head. That was his job.

What is most interesting about Joe's memorable class more than fifty years later—infinitely more relevant than my childish terror—is how remarkably familiar it yet is, especially in settled, well-financed, well-regarded secondary schools provided for America's economically secure families and generally sought after by most families. Some details are now quaint: the segregation by sex, the raised platform, the formality, the individual flip-top wooden desks in rows, the unvarying pedagogy, the considerable fear that a teacher could then provoke. What is remarkable, however, is that so much of the 1946 regimen is still with us.

Most of it is not only recognizable; it is still fully accepted and honored today as a representation of what we call secondary school: a *class* of twenty or so adolescents gathered by age into *grades* to learn *together* a *subject* both for its *content* and for the *skills* embedded in that content taught by a *single teacher* who is responsible for *delivering* that material, assigning *homework*, and *assessing* each student's performance in a uniform manner, all this proceeding in sequential *blocks of time* of forty to sixty minutes each in a specialized *school building* primarily made up of a succession of identical rooms that are used for six hours for fewer than half the days in a year. Joe Barrell would not feel wholly lost in any college preparatory program at any school, public or private, large or small, in Connecticut or beyond, in 2004. This is what *school* is. . . .

Mr. Barrell remains a powerful, if unbeloved, figure for me. Looking back now, he represents some of the glory and much of the misdirection of traditional education.

Barrell was a scholar; he knew his stuff. Academically, he was always a bit over our heads, including those of the Hot Shots, a worthy tactic. He kept the pressure on us to do careful work regularly. The symbols in his little book were evidence that he was paying attention to us, at least as Latin translators, one by one. When a few of us (myself in the lead) were drastically failing he arranged for tutoring from his wife, also a Classics scholar, whose style was warmer and gentler, albeit no less demanding, than was his. Most importantly, even at the cool distance from which he addressed us and from the narrow perch from which he assessed us, he took us seriously.

I can see him now, blue work shirt with wool tie, books orderly before him as he sat at his desk, calm, exhibiting no strong emotion. Most else of what I did in school leaves no such detailed image; I cannot recite even the titles of all the courses that I took. What I remember is selective but stark and detailed, retained not for any abiding joy in the Classics but for the simple reason that Barrell terrified me.

Apart from inflicting the memorable terror, Barrell never led us to invade the Classics deeply, to get beyond the syntax, to see the constancy of humanity in its passions and its terrors, to understand that constancy, and thereby be inspired to grasp the habit of reading serious books from a serious past, to persuade us that immersion in such texts could be a lifelong enriching joy. He rarely ascertained *why* we made a mistake, much less helped us to correct it; he served primarily as a scorekeeper, sorting the proper from the improper. Latin with Barrell was a chore, an annoying but temporary thing like washing dishes supervised by a nitpicky older sister. It was something we had to do because this was School.

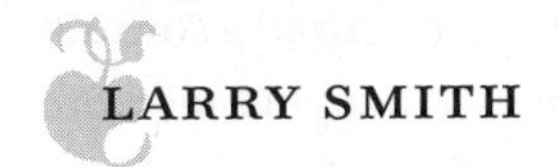

LARRY SMITH

from "My Working-Class Education"

FIRST

In first grade we lined up for everything. Saying the alphabet helped us know our place. I came near the end, I knew that, though I didn't know why. What was order to a kid of five? My memory was a seed garden growing each day as I fed it graham crackers and milk. There was my Roy Rogers pencil box that I forgot at school till someone kept it with its sliding drawer and the good smell of erasers.

So we lined up for everything, like I said—music and gym, lunch and recess, getting on our coats to go home. And one time we stood along the steps at the nurse's office to stand at her lap as she ran a piece of dry spaghetti through our hair. We just didn't ask.

SECOND

Mrs. Reisling spoke to us soft. She was small but we listened to each word—like spiders dancing over waters, coins pressed into our hands. She smelled of flowers in rain when she touched us with our names.

I remember one day seeing myself in the window as I stood at the back sharpening my pencil. She was watching me. I was someone too. I would do good work, lay things out straight, clean up after myself without asking.

THIRD

My third grade teacher, Mrs. Brettel, was my mother's friend, but I was not her child.

She was the one who taught me to love birds, feeding us drawings of them to color each Thursday after gym. These were the birds I watched around our yard each morning and night. And I would rub and rub those crayons into each bird's pale skin till it felt warm and sticky like blood.

I remember how we couldn't believe Mrs. Brettel had a son and a daughter, even though she told us of them. We thought they were story book kids. Then one day she brought the boy to class because he was too sick to go to school and too young to stay home alone. He sat at my desk with me, a quiet brother.

FOURTH

She held my hand as we marched around the gym floor, and her hand wasn't cold or wet like the others, but warm in a way that made me sing inside. Her dress brushed my fingers and I felt myself turn like a bird flying through the sun.

When she moved away, I vanished too. I was a fish without air, a poem without words.

GARY SOTO

Catholics

I was standing in the wastebasket for fighting on the day we received a hunger flag for Biafra. Sister Marie, a tough nun who could throw a softball farther than most men, read a letter that spoke of the grief of that country, looking up now and then to measure our sympathy and to adjust her glasses that had slipped from her nose. She read the three-page letter, placed it on her desk, and walked over to the globe to point out Africa, a continent of constant despair. I craned my neck until, without realizing it, I had one foot out of the wastebasket. Sister Marie turned and stared me back into place, before she went on to lecture us about hunger.

"Hunger is a terrible, terrible thing," she began. "It robs the body of its vitality and the mind of its glory, which is God's."

Sister Marie cruised slowly up and down the rows, tapping a pencil in her palm and talking about death, hunger, and the blessed infants, which were God's, until the students hung their heads in fear or boredom. Then she brightened up.

"With hunger, heavier people would live longer—they have more fat, you see." She tapped her pencil, looked around the room, and pointed to Gloria Leal. "If we didn't have any food whatsoever, Gloria would probably live the longest." Hands folded neatly on her desk, Gloria forced a smile but didn't look around the room at the students who had turned to size her up.

Sister Marie walked up another row, still tapping her pencil and talking about hunger, when she pointed to me. "And Gary . . . well, he would be one of the first to die." Students turned in their chairs to look at me with their mouths open, and I was mad, not for being pointed out but because of that unfair lie. I could outlive the whole class, food or no food. Wasn't I one of the meanest kids in the entire school? Didn't I beat up Chuy Hernandez, a bigger kid? I shook my head in disbelief, and said "nah" under my breath.

Sister Marie glared at me, almost bitterly, as she told the class again that I would be the first one to die. She tapped her pencil as she walked slowly up to me. Scared, I looked away, first up to the ceiling and then to a fly that was walking around on the floor. But my head was snapped up when Sister Marie pushed my chin with her pencil. She puckered her mouth into a clot of lines and something vicious raged in her eyes, like she was getting ready to throw a softball. What it was I didn't know, but I feared that she was going to squeeze me from the wastebasket and hurl me around the room. After a minute or so her face relaxed and she returned to the front of the class where she announced that for the coming three weeks we would collect money daily for Biafra.

"The pagan babies depend on our charitable hearts," she said. She looked around the room and returned to the globe where she again pointed out Africa. I craned my head and pleaded, "Let me see." She stared me back into place and then resumed talking about the fruits of the world, some of which were ours and some of which were not ours.

MICHAEL STEINBERG

High School Baseball Tryouts

I'd been dreaming about this moment since seventh grade. On February 15, over 100 jittery dreamers like me turned out for baseball tryouts in the dingy, grey high school gym. No surprise there. Far Rockaway was the only high school on the peninsula. Which meant that Coach Kerchman always had his pick of the best athletes. More than 250 had tried out for football last fall.

On the first day, Kerchman announced that he had ten spots to fill. Two would be pitchers. Then tryouts began. Standing less than twenty yards away, Mr. K swatted rubber-covered batting-range baseballs at would-be infielders. When he ripped a hard grounder, the rubber-coated ball would skip off the basketball court's polished wooden surface and spin crazily across the floor. If the fielder missed the ball, it would rocket into the gym's brick wall with a loud "thwack," then ricochet back. The terrified rookies, myself among them, watched from the oval running track above the gym, while Imbrianni, Housing, Berman, and Gartner—the veterans who'd already survived this ritual—got to stand right behind the coach, horsing around and heckling the newcomers. While I watched the drill, I couldn't help but wonder what kind of ordeal Kerchman had devised for the new pitchers.

We were the last group to try out. Kerchman placed eight of us in a line across the width of the basketball floor. We each had our own catcher and one varsity hitter to pitch to. There were no nets or batting cages to separate us. No pitching screens to protect us. Kerchman and his veterans stood in safety up on the running track, and when he blew his whistle all the pitchers simultaneously threw to the hitters. It was rough enough trying to concentrate on throwing strikes to varsity hitters, but as soon as you let go with a pitch, line drives and ground balls went whizzing past you. It was a scene right out of a Keystone Kops movie.

The drill of course was *designed* to unnerve you. Your job was to screen out everything else and concentrate on each pitch you threw.

That night, my arm was so sore that I slept with a heating pad wrapped around it. Every hour or so, I'd get up and wander around the house, wondering if I should even bother going back the next day. But when the sun rose, I was eager to get right back at it.

By the last day, my arm throbbed with pain every time I threw a pitch. I had no zip left. I was sure I'd never make the cut. I tried to prepare myself for the worst. At home and in school, I brooded and moped around, continually reassuring myself that I'd done the best I could under the circumstances. I slept in fits and starts. Late at night, a persistent voice would wake me up. "Who would you be without baseball?" it said. "If you don't make it, what will become of you?"

Two days later, Kerchman posted the final squad list. One spot was sure to go to Mark Silverstone, a cocky, Jewish left-hander from Neponsit. I disliked him, yet I envied his arrogance. The first time I went over to his house, he pulled a copy of Machiavelli's *The Prince* off his bookshelf and pointed with pride to a sentence that read, "It's better to be feared than loved." It couldn't have epitomized our differences better. Was he serving me some sort of notice?

A former prep school kid with a chip on his shoulder, Mark was handsome, a good athlete, a ladies' man, and an honor student. Silverstone kissed no one's ass. He was a lot like Kerchman in that way. Either you dealt with him on his terms or he simply ignored you.

My hands were shaking as I scanned the alphabetically listed names. Right below "Silverstone" was "Steinberg." At first, I thought there must be another Steinberg. But when I read my first name, I was too stunned to even speak. My first impulse was to telephone everyone I knew.

I was still a little wobbly when I went over to the equipment cage to pick up my uniform. I could barely wait to hold that jersey in my hands. Lenny Stromeyer, the student manager, scanned his list and abruptly informed me "batting practice pitchers don't get uniforms." Nor, he said, did they travel to road games with the rest of the team. Then came the kicker. "At home games," Lenny said, "your job is to stand at the entrance behind the backstop and chase the foul balls that are hit out of the park."

He was openly gloating—letting me know in no uncertain terms who had more status than whom around here. But who was fat Lenny to be telling me this stuff? My gut burned. A batting practice pitcher? A ball chaser? I wanted to march right into Kerchman's office and protest. But I had to remind myself that he'd cut at least three or four pitchers, all of whom clearly had more talent than I did. I wondered what that was all about.

On the bus ride home, I kept telling myself that at least I'd made the team. I remembered my first season in the P.A.L. league. I was a scrub when the summer began. But by season's end, Coach Bleutrich was so surprised by my progress that he started me in the Queens championship playoffs. Maybe, if I waited my turn and busted my ass in the off-season, the same thing would happen again.

JUDITH GOLD STITZEL

Milk Money

When Mrs. Holland replaced Mrs. Burrell in the middle of the third grade, I couldn't have been happier. Mrs. Burrell never smiled and she told my parents I talked too much. Mrs. Holland looked like one of those pretty blond ladies on the cover of my mother's knitting magazine.

I lived across the street from the school and went home at noon. One of Mrs. Holland's duties was to collect money from the kids who lived too far away and bought milk to go with their bag lunches. Once a week, they put their coins into the brown envelope she sent around the room, and after she got it back, she put it in her desk drawer. Every day, my classmates left their seats two at a time to get their milk and straws from the sturdy metal crate which sat in the middle of her desk, each of its square compartments holding a waxy carton.

Sometimes, one or two cartons remained, and I wondered if someone was absent, or if Mrs. Holland had made a mistake ordering. I wondered why she never asked if someone wanted the leftover milk. I wanted to hold a shiny carton in my hands and roll a slim straw between my fingers. Beyond those yearnings was another. I wanted to know where the milk came from.

Cows, of course. I knew that, even as a city girl, but that's not what made me itch with curiosity. I wanted to know who Mrs. Holland gave that envelope to and who that person gave it to. Were there farmers? Trucks? Truck drivers? Was Mr. Perlmutter, the principal, involved?

Perhaps my concern about these transactions reflected an early interest in commerce. My father and his twin brother owned a junk shop, Gold and Sons, where I could sit at a metal desk in the small office attached to the noisy warehouse. Smudging my wrists and arms on the carbon paper, I'd make out order forms, leaf through ledgers, keep imaginary accounts.

One day, after the other children had returned with their milk, I raised my hand. "What do you do with the money after you collect it?" I asked.

Over the years, different details surface and disappear. Usually I see myself at my wooden chair-desk. Mrs. Holland has walked from behind her desk to stand in front of the class. There are two or three rows of silent children between us, but she seems only inches away. I never remember what I'm wearing. Sometimes, Mrs. Holland wears a black and orange scarf around her neck. Sometimes, I see her thread her right hand through her shoulder-length hair, her fingers long between the strands.

I always hear her.

"How dare you ask me that? What do you think I do with the money?"

She gets larger, moves closer and fills the space between us. The other children disappear.

"Judy Gold," she screams; "Judy Gold, go outside and soak your head. Don't come back until you're ready to apologize."

Soak your head!

Whatever else comes and goes, those three words remain. I didn't understand them when I was eight. I don't understand them now. Why was she so angry at me? Why would I think she took the money?

More upsetting, what was she asking me to do? Confused though I was, I wanted desperately to please her. But how? Where? Should I go to the girls' room? Would I need a hall pass? Did she want me to use the big sink in the basement where the janitor washed out his smelly mops?

I must have left the room and come back again, but I remember neither. Maybe she sent one of my classmates to get me, or came out herself and saw me squatting against the wall, reluctant to sit down on the uncarpeted floor. Maybe when she invited me back in, Mrs. Holland said she was very sorry she had yelled at me. But I would not have forgotten that. As I have not forgotten the milk, my unanswered question, or her inscrutable command.

LAWRENCE SUTIN

One of the Men in the White Coats

Everyone has a science teacher story. Here's mine. It was during the eighth grade, the most painfully raw year of my life. I was changing into an adolescent in public, before my fellow schoolmates. The girls ignored me and the boys used me as a benchmark to gauge how much further they had progressed in physique and sophistication. I was challenged to fights I did not fight. I tried to dress right and had my cool, back-of-the-neck shirt loops ripped routinely when I walked down the hall between classes. When she finally tired of resewing them, my mother simply clipped them off, which felt something like circumcision. As for my teachers at school, I had drawn a spectacularly wretched bunch. My English teacher spent two months on "The Great Stone Face" by Nathaniel Hawthorne, on which I wrote eight tersely lunatic essays, all of which she graded B+. My economics teacher had a smoking habit so intense that he would sit in a glazed trance by the end of the period, waiting like a Pavlovian dog for the bell that would free him to run to the janitorial closet where he kept his smokes until the school hoods began to steal them. But my science teacher was of an altogether different feather. He understood nascent teens with the same precision and indifference as he understood taxonomy. He tossed his scientific knowledge at us with a contempt to which he was entitled in the face of our boredom and scorn. He always wore white gloves and the rumor had passed from year to year that the middle glove finger of his right hand was a fake to mask its loss in a forbidden experiment gone very wrong in his college days. To check that out I constantly watched his right hand. But there was never a definitive movement, or lack thereof, by which I could tell—not that any of my classmates asked for my opinion. As he called on us by pointing (with his index finger) rather than by name, it was a considerable shock to hear him say at the end of the hour (which was also the end of the school day) that Larry Sutin should stay after class. My fellow students smirked or avoided my eyes as they filed out. I walked up to his desk. He raised his right hand in a fist. "This is the only thing that interests you, yes?" I said nothing as he slowly uplifted the middle finger. "See? Now shake." He grabbed my right hand with his and squeezed until my eyes began to water. I didn't think of screaming. It was his room, his school, his hand, his finger biting into mine. "But how can you be sure," he continued, "it's not a padded metal spring in there? Now there's a question. Can you think of an experiment to answer it?" He let go of me, slapped his hand flat on the desk next to a scalpel of the type we used on frogs. "If you cut through the glove and blood spurted out you'd know, wouldn't you?" I closed my eyes to make it all go away. He pressed the scalpel handle into my hand. "Do it. Now!" I opened my eyes. With his left hand he guided my right to the glove finger. I dropped the scalpel. He took it and sliced. The blood and I both ran.

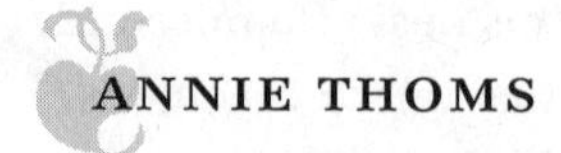

ANNIE THOMS

from With Their Eyes
September 11th—The View from a High School at Ground Zero

I teach high school English four blocks from ground zero. On the morning of September 11th, I walked up the subway stairs and onto Chambers Street, as I do every morning on my way to work. The sky was a bright blue, the day crisp, but as I left the subway station I saw huge clouds of gray smoke hanging in the air above me. The street was filled with people, everybody staring up. So I looked too.

The World Trade Center was on fire, flames leaping from an angry gash in the side of the north tower. I asked the man standing next to me what had happened, and he told me about the planes. The second one, he said, had hit ten minutes earlier. We stood there for a moment, watching papers swirl from the windows of the towers, watching small black objects fall. Then I realized that the small black objects were people. I caught my breath and turned down the hill, toward school.

Stuyvesant High School is four blocks north of the World Trade Center, at the western edge of Manhattan. From its windows, students, faculty, and staff have clear views of the Hudson River, the Statue of Liberty, and, from the south side, the World Trade Center. On September 11th, this meant that hundreds of Stuyvesant students saw the planes hit, saw people jumping from their office windows, saw the towers fall. In less than two hours after the first plane hit the north tower, the school was evacuated—over 3,200 students, faculty, and staff moving safely up the West Side Highway. On that day, and in the weeks that followed, our building became a triage center and base of operations for the rescue and recovery effort. We were out of school for ten days, and then relocated for two weeks to a high school in Brooklyn before resuming classes in our building in October.

Stuyvesant is a magnet school, drawing high-achieving students from all five boroughs of New York City. This makes for a diverse student body, but it also made it difficult, after September 11th, for students and faculty to meet as a community—public transportation was disrupted, and our one common neighborhood had been taken away. September 11th was the fifth day of classes of a new year; we had barely learned each other's names, and suddenly we were all separated.

As a teacher, one of the hardest things about the first days after the attacks was being completely cut off from my students. I felt helpless, unable to talk to them, unable to use my classroom as a place to share our experiences and process some of what had happened to us. At home, I wrote. I contacted relatives and friends, I watched TV, I cried. One of my colleagues, from her home in Brooklyn, alerted me to a couple of student-run websites where Stuyvesant students were talking to each other, posting hundreds of messages about their own experiences on the day of the attacks, and their reactions since then. Reading their accounts, I was struck by the number of different stories they told, and the strength of their need to tell those stories. An idea began to form.

Late last year, I had become the faculty advisor for the Stuyvesant Theater Community. In that position, I knew I would be responsible for this year's winter drama. What if, I thought, we created a play in which Stuyvesant students were able to tell their own stories, and the stories of others in our community, about our experiences on September 11th?

I looked to the work of playwright and actress Anna Deavere Smith, especially her plays *Fires in the Mirror*, which focuses on the aftermath of the 1991 Crown Heights riots, and *Twilight: Los Angeles*, which explores the issues surrounding the L.A. riots of 1992. For each of these plays, Smith interviewed hundreds of people on tape, creating monologues from their spoken words. She then performed in the character and voice of the people she had interviewed, producing in each one-woman show a vivid, complex picture of a community's reaction to violent tragedy.

This format, with a larger cast, seemed ideal for our situation. I broached the idea to the Stuyvesant Theater Community Slate, and together we decided to try it out. In late November, we chose a student director and two student producers.

We set out to assemble a cast which would represent the diversity of our school—Stuyvesant is over 50 percent Asian and just over 40 percent white, with the remaining number made up of black and Latino students. Many of our students are immigrants or first-generation Americans. We visited a number of Stuyvesant's cultural clubs, and put out the word that we were looking for cast members from all four grades. Of the forty-five or so students who auditioned, reading monologues from *Fires in the Mirror*, we chose ten. They were five boys and five girls; they were white, black, Asian, and Middle Eastern; they were immigrants and kids born in New York City. Few of them had acted at Stuyvesant before; in a school of over three thousand students, few knew each other at all.

At our first meeting, the atmosphere in the room was a little strained. We did ice-breaking introductions, and then moved into our first brainstorming session: Who should the actors interview? We came up with a list of specific names and of general categories: Liz wanted to interview "a freshman nobody knows"; several of us wanted the perspective of a Muslim student; actors called out names of friends they thought would give great interviews. Ilena read the completed list aloud, and the cast wrote down their top choices, including students, faculty, and building staff.

Each cast member then set out with a small tape recorder to interview two or three people. Following Anna Deavere Smith's example, we did not limit the actors to playing only characters of their own race or gender. The people each actor interviewed were the people he or she played, regardless of their physical dissimilarity. Each interviewee was offered the option of remaining anonymous; several did.

It was important to all of us that the play not be focused exclusively on the events of September 11th, but also address the days, weeks, and months afterward. Because we wanted to elicit stories about a variety of subjects, the actors did not ask all their interviewees the same questions, though there were some common ones: Where were you on September 11th, and what did you see? Have we gotten back to normal? What's "normal" to you? What do you think we need to talk about? . . .

Our first rehearsal with the completed monologues took place in the theater in mid-December. . . . The listening was intense. In interviewing, and in editing, each story had been alone, singular. Now, we heard the stories speak to each other, painting a picture of anger and panic, of hope and strength, of humor and resilience. During and after each new monologue, we teared up, laughed, wiped our eyes. For each of us, there were lines in one or two monologues that sounded utterly familiar—things we had said, or thought, ourselves. For each of us, there were details and reactions we had never thought of before. When the last monologue had finished, we sat and looked at each other, amazed. . . .

In rehearsal, as in creating the monologues, there was a lot of individual work before we brought the show together as a whole. Each actor listened to his or her audiotapes over and over, capturing the rhythms and vocal patterns of each interviewee, and practicing the interviewee's stance and mannerisms. We were aware from the outset of the fine line between portrayal and caricature, especially in the case of "You Need Hope," for which Marcel had interviewed two students from P.S. 721, the special education school within Stuyvesant. Marcel spoke with the families of the students, and researched ways to portray them accurately and without offending anyone. Other actors did field work to prepare themselves for performance: Shanleigh skipped lunch to sit in on Matt Polazzo's social studies class several days in a row, taking notes on his walk. For every actor in the show, the prospect of having their interviewees come to see themselves played on stage was a little daunting. . . .

Despite our focus on bringing out stories which had not yet been heard, many members of the Stuyvesant community were opposed to the idea of a play about September 11th. They felt that there had been enough talk about the day, enough talk about our reactions—they wanted to move on. Some of them came to the play; some did not. We performed *with their eyes* on February 8th and 9th, 2002, to an audience which included friends from outside Stuyvesant and members of several media organizations. Both shows were received with standing ovations.

I've been asked many times over the past six months how the Stuyvesant community is doing, how we have recovered. There is no easy answer. We are more than 3,200 students, teachers, and building staff—there are as many reactions as there are people in the building. Each of us knows our own story: where we were on September 11th, what we thought, how it has changed us. Each of us knows the stories of our friends. But even within a single building, there are thousands of stories waiting to be heard.

March 2002

JANE TOMPKINS

Reverie

In my mind's eye I keep seeing rows. Rows of desks, running horizontal across a room, light yellow wooden tops, pale beige metal legs, a shallow depression for pencils at the far edge, and chairs of the same material, separate from the desks, movable. The windows—tall and running the length of the classroom—are on the left. Light streams through.

The rows are empty.

Now the desks darken and curve. They're made of older grainier wood; they're the kind with a surface that comes out from the back of the seat on your right and wraps around in front. The desk top is attached to the seat where you sit, which is clamped to the seats on either side or to those in front and in back. The desks metamorphose in my mind. Now they are hinged, tops brown and scarred; they open to reveal notebooks, textbooks covered in the shiny green-and-white book covers of Glen Rock Junior High; there's a bottle of mucilage and a pink eraser. On top, there's a hole for an inkwell, black and empty. The seat, when you stand, folds up behind.

Sometimes the desks are movable; more often they're clamped down. Always they're in rows. And empty. The teacher's place is empty, too, another desk, or table-like thing. Sometimes it's a podium on a platform. The blackboard behind.

The scenes are all mixed together—grade school with graduate school—but always the windows along one side of the room, and always the desks in rows.

After babyhood we spend a lot of time learning to sit in rows. Going from unruly to ruled. Learning to write on pages that are lined. Learning to obey. There is no other way, apparently. Even if the desks were arranged in a circle, or were not desks at all but chairs or ottomans, still they would have to form some pattern. We would have to learn to sit still and listen.

The first part of life goes on for a long time. The habit of learning to sit in rows doesn't leave off when the rows themselves are gone. Having learned to learn the rules, you look for them everywhere you go, to avoid humiliation. You learn to find your seat in the invisible rows.

The last part of life, though, is different. It is no longer automatic, your walking in and sitting down. When you see a row, your gorge rises, or you are simply indifferent. When the command comes to be seated, you don't obey. All of a sudden, survival no longer depends on getting to your desk in the ten seconds after the buzzer sounds. It depends on listening only to your inner monitor, which says: You'd better go while the going's good. Time to give up the security of rows.

'Cause you're not *in* the classroom anymore. There is no blackboard with equations on it, no teacher with her pointer to point out what you need to know. No test, no assignment. No three o'clock when the bell for dismissal rings. No after school.

No smell of chalk dust and freshly sharpened pencils, no fragrances of different kinds of paper, gray and white and yellow, blank pages, lined and unlined, inviting you to prove something, yourself . . . I can do this problem, spell that word, name the capital of that country, explain the meaning of that term.

Though there was always fear associated with sitting in rows—am I too different? will I pass the test? does anybody like me?—the desks and chairs and tasks provided an escape from fear by giving me something definite to do. Add the column of figures. Learn the causes of the war.

Now, wandering the world outside of school, having transcended "rows," nothing to do, no place to go, I am terrified. In the huge, dark, unfurnished world without rows, I cower and tremble. Give me back Mrs. Colgan. Let me be in 1B again. Let me learn to add, to subtract, to carry, and to borrow numbers. Give me a problem to do.

I see the light-filled classrooms, rows on rows, desks, chairs, waiting to be filled: let the lesson begin. "Our first assignment will be to learn the periodic table." Let me back in. Please. Let me sit down again, open my notebook to the first blank page, start writing. When is the exam?

BRUCE WEIGL

Before and After

There was a before and then there was an after. There were many small befores, and one irrevocable after.

On June 6, 1967, I graduated into the humid, slag-heavy air from the Admiral Ernest J. King High School. My mother and my father were there. My Yugoslav grandmother Anna Grassa wanted her picture taken with me. My sister was there. I can hardly imagine them. I did not have a sense of the heaviness of their bodies.

Our valedictorian made a grand speech, primarily about his own accomplishments. No one liked him. My chums and I sat in the back and made noises with our hands that sounded like flatulence. In the small space between two names being called out over the public address system, we made cups with our hands and added other names, names that were jokes, like Manual Labor or Who Flung Poo. This was in the before when we believed that laughing out loud could save you from the hard facts of a wasted life.

After we got our diplomas, Pat, Rab, Bill, Hank, and I headed out in Bill's car for some liquor to celebrate. We got this older guy who worked at the Slovenian Club to buy us bottles of cheap sweet wine in exchange for a fifth for himself. I swear to Christ we turned the heater of the car up as high as it would go and blasted the fan with all of the windows rolled up and drank that shit through straws until we were somehow even more stupid than before we had started drinking.

With these boys who loved me first and best the way boys loved then, I spent my last six days of a life we had no way of knowing was being ripped terribly away from us. We dared our sweat-sheened bodies at each other. We slept together those last days before my departure and ate and drank together and took of each other's food and beer and wine. They were trying to bring me into some kind of circle, but I pulled away.

In the before, on the night before my departure, I drove restlessly down the back streets of Lorain that I had memorized as if there were a door that had been there all along that I could find now and slide through and escape into another life where the stars would not explode in my face.

Then I went back to my chums who did not dare say the brutally simple good-byes but drank hard with me and touched me in their drunkenness and in the after, months later, lives later, leeches and rot and words like a ball of steel in my mouth, I would lie with another boy in the razor grass, his stomach torn open and glistening in the light breaking through the canopies of green, and I would remember those boys of my last nights in the world, their grace undone now, and then I would lose them forever in a war's wind swirling and give myself to the dying boy who begged me, above the liftship blast, not to tell his mother that he had died this way.

MEREDITH SUE WILLIS

What I Learned in First Grade

When I was small, I used to make up stories about freedom-loving wild horses and brave Indian princesses. Sometimes I wrote these down, often in the form of comic books, but I never wrote directly about my own life experiences until I was thirteen and recorded for posterity how much I had hated first grade. When my mother read that piece, she was shocked. She said she always assumed that because I was *good* at school I must *like* it.

I had looked forward to starting school. School was our family business: my father was a high school science teacher, and my mother had been a teacher too, although she stayed at home with me and my baby sister. That's what women did then, and she considered housekeeping a high moral calling. She indicated that it was a sign of righteousness to give up nice clothes and a salary to stay home and iron. She hated ironing, but said it was especially important to do the things you like least.

School, my father's domain, sounded better to me. Daddy came home every day and told us stories about school: he had tales of his colleagues' foibles and his students' struggles; he had a human tapeworm in a jar; he had jokes from *The Readers' Digest* to keep his afternoon classes awake. I think I expected first grade to be my father's world.

We walked nearly a mile to the Shinnston Grade School, from East Shinnston into town, along a brick sidewalk, past houses, past undeveloped fields. Coal trucks rattled by. After a while, the houses came closer together, and the grade school stood in front of us, a long brick block with tall windows and high ceilings. It smelled of floor oil and bag lunches. All the first grade classes were on the main floor, Miss Shreve and Miss Radford to the left and Miss Oliverio to the right. Forty of us sat in desks bolted to the floor. Our most important activity, as I remember it, was holding still, not an easy lesson for six-year-old bodies used to running, climbing, and curling up at will.

My mother and father told me that my teacher, Miss Shreve, was the best one because she was so strict. Miss Radford next door was strict too, and the two of them had gone about as far as an unmarried woman could go in the work world in those days. They were straight-backed and pigeon-breasted, and wore what would later be called power suits. They had their hair done at the beauty parlor every week. They could, either one of them, have run a corporation or a banana republic.

At the other end of the floor was Miss Oliverio, also professionally coifed and neatly suited, but there were rumors that she was easy on kids. That she gave out treats. That she hugged the littlest ones when they cried. This seemed somehow to be related to the fact that she was Italian, as if being Italian gave you, along with a propensity for pierced ears and cooking with garlic, an unprofessional tendency to be kind to children.

I understood that control over children was an essential part of the teacher's job. Like a child who identifies with the union because his dad is a shop steward, I understood that I was supposed to be on the teachers' side. In practice, what this meant was that I was excruciatingly attentive to following Miss Shreve's instructions. I was terrified of getting paddled, but mostly I wanted to be a good student. Therefore, when she told us to put our heads on our desks and keep quiet, I did precisely that.

Sometimes Miss Shreve had to go out, to the bathroom I suppose, or for a smoke, and Miss Radford would stand in the doorway and watch us and her class, too. We were even more afraid of Miss Radford than of Miss Shreve because Miss Radford paddled you and then made you sit in the wastebasket. But sometimes, no one watched us. It didn't take long for most of the kids to figure out when we were really alone and start buzzing and twisting in their seats and making faces and giggling and whispering, and some even got up and made breathless forays up and down the aisles. But I kept my head down. The boy who sat behind me would tap me with his finger and say my name over and over, urgently trying to get me to join in the fun, but I kept my face pressed into my arms.

Occasionally Miss Shreve also told us to put our heads down when she was in the room. Maybe she wanted to do her grade book or look out the window. Maybe she thought we needed a rest. One day she said, "All right, class, that's enough. Put your heads on your seats."

Always before she had said, Put your heads on your desks. I don't know why she changed that day; it was perhaps merely the human desire for a break in routine. I was puzzled, but determined to follow orders. The other kids were, as usual, cradling their heads on top of their desks. But I got down on my knees on the splintery oiled wood floor and put my head on the varnished seat, still warm from my behind.

The room became unusually quiet.

She had been pacing in the front, but I heard her stop short, reverse direction, and come up the aisle toward me.

I looked out from under my arm and saw her sturdy two-inch heels and the nylons on her well-shaped calves that seemed too young for her face. When she got to me, she stopped, and I looked over her skirt, over her crossed arms, to the grimacing yellow teeth and the purple splotches of rage on her cheeks.

"Meredith," she said, in a voice like a jackhammer, "exactly *what* do you think you are doing?"

That was when it struck me that the other children, who I *knew* were not nearly as good as I was, had done the right thing, and I hadn't. It was one of those breathtaking flashes of bright comprehension, an epiphany: *doing exactly as you are told can be dangerous too*.

"Get up into that chair!" she shouted. "Right now! Don't you dare make fun of me! Get your little behind into that chair!"

She didn't hit me—maybe she didn't trust herself in her fury, or maybe she saw in my eyes that there had been a terrible mistake. It didn't stop her from being angry, but she didn't hit me. Another time, she smacked every hand in the entire class with a ruler, including mine, but by then, I was entertaining the possibility that she was a tyrant, and that it was unfair to hit everyone if a few misbehaved.

I also discovered in the coming months that, if I did my work quickly and neatly and sat very still, I could escape first grade. My body would be there, but my mind would follow some graceful imaginary figure who danced on the chalkboard ledge and then passed through the window glass into the open air.

By second grade, I had begun to draw what I was seeing in the margins of my papers. They didn't let you read books in my school, but I found that, during the spelling and grammar drills and during handwriting practice, I could hold onto the thread of my stories of wild horses and great battles with evil that were won by heroic girls.

I don't think it would have destroyed my imagination to have been in Miss Oliverio's happy class; I don't think it would have been destroyed if I had been in a school where you could sit on pillows in a reading nook or go to the science corner and chart the growth of tadpoles.

But we live the lives we have, and I learned the discipline of imagination in first grade, which, while not necessarily the best thing, was what happened to me.

Notes on Contributors

SHERMAN ALEXIE is the author of ten books, most recently a novel, *Indian Killer*, and a collection of poems, *The Summer of Black Widows*. His book *Reservation Blues* won an American Book Award from the Before Columbus Foundation. Alexie is also the author of *The Lone Ranger and Tonto Fistfight in Heaven*, which served as the basis for his screenplay for the film *Smoke Signals*, winner of two Sundance Film Festival awards in 1998. Sherman Alexie is a Spokane and Coeur d'Alene Indian from Wellpinit, Washington.

MAGGIE ANDERSON is the author of five books of poems, most recently *Windfall: New and Selected Poems*. She is the coeditor of *Learning by Heart: Contemporary American Poetry about School* and of *A Gathering of Poets*, a collection of poems commemorating the twentieth anniversary of the shooting of students in an antiwar protest on the campus of Kent State University in 1970. Anderson directs the Wick Poetry Center at Kent State University in Kent, Ohio, and the Northeast Ohio Master of Fine Arts in Creative Writing program. She taught poetry in elementary and secondary schools and in correctional facilities and rehabilitation centers in West Virginia, Pennsylvania, and Ohio from 1977 to 1989.

RANE ARROYO is a Puerto Rican and midwestern writer who writes in many genres. His most recent poetry collection is *The Portable Fame*, and his first fiction collection is *How to Name a Hurricane*. Arroyo went through Chicago's elementary school system slowly learning English, and he worked as a program associate for Urban Gateways in Chicago, teaching and hiring residency artists for Chicago public schools. Arroyo now teaches English and creative writing at the University of Toledo in Toledo, Ohio.

ESTHER ROYER AYERS was born in 1938 into an Old Order Mennonite family and grew up in a farming community in the outskirts of Columbiana, Ohio. Unlike most Old Order Mennonite children whose education ends at eighth grade, Ayers was allowed to attend high school and later college at the University of Arkansas at Little Rock. Her first book, *Rolling Down Black Stockings: A Passage Out of the Old Order Mennonite Religion*, was published in 2005.

PHYLLIS BARBER'S most recent book is *Parting the Veil: Stories from a Mormon Imagination*. Her memoir, *How I Got Cultured: A Nevada Memoir*, won the Associated Writing Programs Award in creative nonfiction in 1992 and was also named the best autobiography of that year by the Association for Mormon Letters. Barber is on the faculty at the Vermont College MFA in Writing Program.

JAN BEATTY'S first book, *Mad River*, won the 1995 Agnes Lynch Starrett Prize. Her most recent collection of poems is *Boneshaker*. For the past twelve years, Beatty has hosted and produced *Prosody*, a public radio show on NPR affiliate WYEP-FM, featuring the work of national writers. She has taught in the International Poetry Forum's Poets-in-Person program in Pittsburgh, Pennsylvania, high schools and she currently teaches creative writing at Carlow University.

MARK BRAZAITIS is the author of *The River of Lost Voices: Stories from Guatemala*, winner of the 1998 Iowa Short Fiction Award, *Steal My Heart*, a novel, and *An American Affair*, a short story collection that won the 2004 George Garrett Fiction Award. Brazaitis taught English at a junior high school in Guatemala during his three years in the Peace Corps. Currently he teaches English and creative writing at West Virginia University in Morgantown, West Virginia.

CHRISTOPHER BUCKLEY'S most recent book of poems is *And the Sea*. He is also the author of two books of creative nonfiction, most recently *Sleep Walk*. Buckley is the editor of *Homage to Vallejo* and *A Condition of the Spirit: The Life and Work of Larry Levis*. After graduating from St. Mary's College, he taught seventh and eighth grades in a parochial school in Torrance, California. Buckley currently teaches in the creative writing program at the University of California, Riverside.

DAVID CITINO is the author of ten books, including the *Book of Appassionata: Collected Poems*, *Broken Symmetry,* and *The Weight of the Heart.* He is also the author of a memoir, *Paperwork.* At the time of his death in 2005, Citino was working on a children's book about baseball. A member of the creative writing faculty at Ohio State University in Columbus, Ohio, Citino also participated in reading and writing programs from the elementary level through high school and gave workshops for teachers throughout Ohio.

ROBERT COLES is the James Agee Professor of Social Ethics at Harvard University and professor of psychiatry and medical humanities at Harvard Medical School. He is the author of more than fifty books, including the Pulitzer Prize–winning *Children of Crisis*. For twenty years, Coles has taught a seminar for new teachers called "Writers in the Classroom" for the Harvard Graduate School of Education. The texts used in this course are included in his anthology, *Teaching Stories: An Anthology on the Power of Learning and Literature.*

KATIE DALEY is a poet, performer, and teacher living in Cleveland, Ohio. She leads writing workshops at schools, universities, and writers' festivals around the country. Since 2001, Daley has also been touring her one-woman show of poetic monologues, *Full Blast Alive: Voices from the Ruby Side* to theaters, schoolrooms, and night clubs in the U.S. and in Canada.

TOI DERRICOTTE is the author of four books of poems, including *Captivity* and *Tender*. Her nonfiction work, *The Black Notebooks* was the winner of the 1998 Anisfield-Wolf Award and a *New York Times* Notable Book of the Year. With Cornelius Eady, she founded and implemented Cave Canem, the first historic workshop and retreat for African American poets. Derricotte currently teaches creative writing at the University of Pittsburgh in Pittsburgh, Pennsylvania.

ANNIE DILLARD'S *Pilgrim at Tinker Creek* won the Pulitzer Prize for general nonfiction in 1975. She is the author of twelve other books, including the memoir *An American Childhood*, the novel *The Living*, and *Teaching a Stone to Talk*, a collection of essays which was judged one of the best books of the 1980s by the

Boston Globe. Her most recent book is a nonfiction narrative, *For the Time Being*.

MARK DOTY'S most recent book of poems is *School for the Arts*. He is also the author of two memoirs, *Heaven's Coast* and *Firebird,* and a book of short essays, *Still Life with Oysters and Lemon.* Before teaching creative writing at various universities, Doty worked as a Head Start teacher, a preschool teacher, a Before-and-After School program teacher, director of a federally funded day care center, and a poet-in-residence in the Iowa Artists-in-the-Schools program.

VIOLET A. DUTCHER teaches rhetoric and composition and writing courses at Eastern Mennonite University in Virginia. Previously, she taught writing and women's studies courses at Kent State University, where she established community partnerships between university students and local elementary schools and nursing homes. Dutcher has published articles in *Feminism(s), Mennonite Weekly Review*, and *Magistra: A Journal of Women's Spirituality in History*.

JOYCE DYER is the author of two nonfiction books, *In a Tangled Wood: An Alzheimer's Journey* and *Gum-Dipped: A Daughter Remembers Rubber Town.* She is also the editor of *Bloodroot: Reflections on Place by Appalachian Women Writers,* which won the 1998 Appalachian Studies Award. Currently, Dyer is the director of the Lindsay-Crane Center for Writing and Literature at Hiram College in Hiram, Ohio, where she also holds the John S. Kenyon Chair in English.

LINDA DYER is the author of *Fictional Teeth*, a collection of poems. She was a first place and second place winner in the 1995 *San Francisco Bay Guardian* Poetry Contest. Dyer passed away in San Francisco, California, in July 2006.

KATHY EVANS'S most recent book of poems is *Hunger and Sorrow*. She is also the author of *Imagination Comes to Breakfast* and *As the Heart Is Held*. Evans has taught writing workshops to children and adults of all ages through the California Poets-in-the-Schools program and WritersCorps and currently teaches incarcerated youth at Marin County Juvenile Hall.

HENRY LOUIS GATES, JR. is the author of *The Signifying Monkey: Towards a Theory of Afro-American Literary Criti-*

cism, which won both a 1989 American Book Award and an Anisfield-Wolf Book Award for Race Relations. The writer and producer of several documentary series for PBS, most recently "African American Lives," he is also the author of *Colored People: A Memoir*, which won the Heartland Prize for Nonfiction. Gates is widely recognized for his extensive research on African American history and literature and for bringing to preeminence the African American Studies program at Harvard University, where he is the Alphonse Fletcher University Professor and the Director of the W. E. B. Du Bois Institute for African and African American Research. In 1997 Gates was voted one of *Time* magazine's "25 Most Influential Americans."

DIANE GILLIAM is the author of three books of poems, *Recipe for Blackberry Cake*, *One of Everything*, and, most recently, *Kettle Bottom*, which won the Ohioana Library Association Book of the Year Award in Poetry in 2005. *Kettle Bottom* was also an American Booksellers' Association Book Sense Pick for the Top Ten Poetry Books of 2005. Gilliam currently teaches creative writing and Appalachian literature at Converse College in Spartanburg, South Carolina.

RICHARD HAGUE is the author of twelve collections of poetry and prose, including *Milltown Natural: Essays and Stories from a Life* and the multi-genre *Lives of the Poem: Community and Connection in a Writing Life*, which chronicles his work over three decades among young people and adults. Since 1969, he has taught English and creative writing at Purcell Marian High School in Cincinnati, Ohio.

DAVID HASSLER is the author of two books of poems, most recently *Red Kimono, Yellow Barn*, for which he was named the 2006 Ohio Poet of the Year. He is the coeditor of *Learning by Heart: Contemporary American Poetry about School* and *A Place to Grow: Voices and Images of Urban Gardeners*. With photographer Gary Harwood, he is the author of *Growing Season: The Life of a Migrant Community*, a photographic documentary with first-person narratives based on interviews with Mexican American migrant farm workers. Hassler is the program and outreach director for the Wick Poetry Center at Kent State University, where he teaches an undergraduate service-learning course, Teaching Poetry in the Schools, and conducts writing workshops for students, teachers, and seniors in northeast Ohio.

RUTH ELLA HENDRICKS teaches art to children in kindergarten through eighth grade in Pittsburgh, Pennsylvania. She also leads an after-school program involving a team of teachers and para-educators who work with seventy students on homework assignments, computer skills, swimming, knitting, and exercise.

WILLIAM HEYEN'S sixteen books of poems include *The Confessions of Doc Williams and Other Poems*, *Crazy Horse in Stillness*, *The Swastika Poems*, and *Shoah Train*, a finalist for the 2004 National Book Award. He is also the author of five books of essays and the editor of several anthologies, including *September 11, 2001: American Writers Respond*. Heyen has taught junior high school and supervised student teachers of English. He is professor of English and Poet-in-Residence Emeritus at SUNY Brockport.

FAITH S. HOLSAERT was raised by two mothers in a biracial 1950s household and attended New York City's Little Red School House. She registered voters in southwest Georgia in 1962 and later moved to the coalfields of southern West Virginia, where she taught public school and supported the Black Lung and Welfare Rights Movements. Holsaert has published short fiction in several journals including *Fugue*, *Redbook*, and *Arable* and is the author of a chapbook, *While We Were Singing*.

HANK HUDEPOHL is the author of a book of poetry, *The Journey of Hands*. His poems have appeared in several journals, including *Limestone*, *Cargoes*, *Appalachian Heritage*, *Ghoti*, and *Image/Word*, a book of ekphrastic poems by the Randolph-Macon Maier Museum of Art. Hudepohl has taught writing courses at the University of Kentucky and at Hollins University, where he was assistant poetry editor of *The Hollins Critic* from 2004 to 2006.

LAWSON FUSAO INADA is a third-generation Japanese American from Fresno, California. During World War II he and his family were interned in camps in California, Arkansas, and Colorado. He is the author of three collections of poems, *Draw-*

ing the Line, *Before the War*, and *Legends from Camp*, which received both the Oregon Book Award and the American Book Award in 1997. From 1988 to 1998 Inada was a member of the Committee on Racism and Bias in the Teaching of English for the National Council of Teachers of English. He taught for many years at Southern Oregon University.

JULIA SPICHER KASDORF'S most recent book of poetry is *Eve's Striptease*. Her first book, *Sleeping Preacher*, won the Agnes Lynch Starrett Prize in 1991. She is also the author of *The Body and the Book: Writing from a Mennonite Life*, and a biography, *Fixing Tradition: Joseph W. Yoder, Amish-American*. Kasdorf has developed the Writer in the Community project at Pennsylvania State University, where she also teaches creative writing and women's studies.

GARRISON KEILLOR is an author, storyteller, performance artist, poet, and comedian. He has published three books for children and eight books for adults, including *Lake Wobegon Days*, *We Are Still Married*, and *Wobegon Boy*. His most recent book is *Homegrown Democrat*. In addition, he writes poetry and has edited several poetry collections, including *Good Poems*. Keillor is best known as the founder and host of the Minnesota Public Radio show, *A Prairie Home Companion*, which he has hosted since 1974.

JANE KENYON'S *Collected Poems* was published posthumously in 2005. During her lifetime, she published four collections of poetry and a book of translation, *Twenty Poems of Anna Akhmatova*. She is also the author of *A Hundred White Daffodils: Essays, Interviews, the Akhmatova Translations, Newspaper Columns, and One Poem*. Kenyon was featured with her husband, Donald Hall, in the Emmy Award–winning Bill Moyers special, "A Life Together." At the time of her death in 1995, Kenyon was New Hampshire's Poet Laureate.

JESSE LEE KERCHEVAL is the author of nine books, including the poetry collections *Dog Angel* and *World as Dictionary*. She is also the author of the story collections *Alice in Dairyland*, which won the 2006 Prairie Schooner Book Prize, and *The Dogeater*, which won the 1987 Associated Writing Programs Award in Short Fiction. Her memoir, *Space*, about growing up near Cape Kennedy during the race for the moon, won the Alex Award from the American Library Association. Kercheval is also the author of a textbook on creative writing, *Building Fiction*, and is the Sally Mead Hands Bascom Professor of English at the University of Wisconsin, where she directs the Wisconsin Institute for Creative Writing.

BARBARA KINGSOLVER is the author of many books of fiction, poetry, and essays, including *Small Wonder* and the best-selling *High Tide in Tucson: Essays from Now and Never*. Her novels include *The Bean Trees*, *Prodigal Summer*, *Animal Dreams*, and *The Poisonwood Bible*, which won the National Book Prize of South Africa and was an Oprah's Book Club selection. In 2000 Kingsolver was awarded the National Humanities Medal, our nation's highest honor for service through the arts.

LEONARD KRESS is the author of three poetry collections, *The Centralia Mine Fire*, *Sappho's Apples*, and *Orphics*. He teaches art history, religion, philosophy, and writing at Owens College in northwest Ohio. Kress spent almost a decade as a substitute teacher in the Philadelphia, Pennsylvania, schools—everything from kindergarten to vocational high school.

STEPHEN KUUSISTO'S memoir, *Planet of the Blind*, was a *New York Times* Notable Book of the Year for 1998. His most recent memoir is *Eavesdropping: A Life by Ear*. He is also the author of a book of poems, *Only Bread, Only Light*. Kuusisto teaches in the disability studies program at Ohio State University in Columbus, Ohio, where he also serves as a fellow of the Moritz College of Law's Center for Interdisciplinary Law and Policy Studies. He speaks widely on diversity, disability, education, and public policy, and he and his dog, Vidal, visit public schools on a regular basis.

PHILIP LEVINE is the author of sixteen books of poetry, most recently *Breath*. His other poetry collections include *Ashes* and *What Work Is*, both of which won the National Book Award, and *The Simple Truth*, which was awarded the 1994 Pulitzer Prize. Levine has also published a memoir *The Bread of Time: Toward an Autobiography*. In 2000 Levine was elected a chancellor of the Academy of American Poets.

AUDRE LORDE was a member of the Harlem Writers' Guild, founded by John Henrik Clarke, while a student at Hunter College High School in New York City. With Barbara Smith, Lorde cofounded Kitchen Table: Women of Color Press. The author of ten books of poems and five books of prose, Lorde worked as a librarian for eight years before beginning her teaching career. At the time of her death in 1992, she was Thomas Hunter Professor of English at Hunter College and was named New York State Poet. *The Collected Poems of Audre Lorde* was published posthumously in 1998.

PETER MARKUS is the author of four books, most recently *Good Brother* and *The Singing Fish*. His poetry and fiction have appeared in many anthologies, including *American Poetry: The Next Generation* and *New Sudden Fiction*. He has been a writer-in-residence at Interlochen Center for the Arts and at the Michigan Youth Arts Festival and conducts workshops through the PEN/Faulkner National Writers-in-the-Schools program and the Gotham Writers' Workshop. Currently, Markus is the senior writer with the InsideOut Literary Arts Project in Detroit, Michigan, a writer-in-the-schools organization that places poets and fiction writers into 23 inner-city Detroit schools.

REBECCA McCLANAHAN'S most recent book is a collection of memoir-based essays, *The Riddle Song and Other Rememberings*, which won the 2005 Glasgow Prize from *Shenandoah*. She has also published four volumes of poetry, most recently *Naked as Eve*, and three books about writing, including *Word Painting: A Guide to Writing More Descriptively*. She has taught elementary and high school English and, for fifteen years, was writer-in-residence for Charlotte-Mecklenburg schools in North Carolina. She currently teaches in the low-residency MFA program of Queens University.

KENNETH A. McCLANE, the W. E. B. Du Bois Professor of Literature at Cornell University, is the author of seven poetry collections, including *Take Five: Collected Poems 1971–1986*, and a volume of personal essays, *Walls: Essays 1985–1990*. His work has been reprinted in *The Best American Essays*. He attended the Collegiate School, America's oldest independent school, founded in 1628. Collegiate is all-male, and McClane was the second African American to be a student there.

BRENDA MILLER is the author of *Season of the Body*, which was a finalist for the PEN American Center Book Award in Creative Nonfiction. She has received four Pushcart Prizes and coauthored, with Suzanne Paola, the textbook, *Tell it Slant: Writing and Shaping Creative Nonfiction*. Miller teaches English at Western Washington University in Bellingham, Washington, and is the editor-in-chief of the *Bellingham Review*.

NAOMI SHIHAB NYE is the author of many books of poems, including *You and Yours*, which received the 2005 Isabella Gardner Poetry Award. Born to a Palestinian father and an American mother, Nye is also well known for her essays and anthologies of the Middle East, including the award-winning *This Same Sky* and *Different Ways to Pray*. She is also the author of a collection of essays, *Never in a Hurry: Essays on People and Places*. Nye has been working as an itinerant writer-in-the-schools and visiting writer-at-large for the past thirty-years. She is featured on two PBS poetry specials: "The Language of Life with Bill Moyers" and "The United States of Poetry."

GREGORY ORR is the author of nine books of poems, including *Concerning the Book That Is the Body of the Beloved*, *The Caged Owl: New and Selected Poems*, and *Orpheus and Eurydice*. His memoir, *The Blessing*, was chosen by *Publishers Weekly* as one of the fifty best books of 2002. Orr is also the author of a book about poetry, *Poetry as Survival*. He teaches creative writing at the University of Virginia in Charlottesville, Virginia.

VIVIAN GUSSIN PALEY writes and teaches about the world of young children, examining their stories and play, their logic and their thinking for meaning in the social and moral landscapes of classroom life. A kindergarten teacher for thirty-seven years, Paley is the author of twelve books about education, most recently *A Child's Work: The Importance of Fantasy Play* and *In Mrs. Tully's Room: A Childcare Portrait*. In 2004, Paley was named Outstanding Educator in the Language Arts by the National Council of Teachers of English.

MAJ RAGAIN is the author of five books of poems, including *Twist the Axe: A Horseplayer's Story*, *Burley Dark One Sucker*

Fired, Fresh Oil Loose Gravel, and *A Hungry Ghost Surrenders His Tackle Box*. After being struck by polio in 1949, Ragain was home-schooled from grades four through eight. Currently, Ragain teaches creative writing at Kent State University and hosts a monthly poetry reading at the North Water Street Gallery in Kent, Ohio.

ALBERTO RÍOS is the author of nine books of poetry, including *The Theater of Night, The Smallest Muscle in the Human Body*, a finalist for the 2002 National Book Award, and *Whispering to Fool the Wind*, winner of the 1991 Walt Whitman Award. He is also the author of two short story collections and the memoir *Capirotada: A Nogales Memoir*. Ríos teaches creative writing and Latin American literature at Arizona State University in Tempe, Arizona, where he is the Regents Professor of English.

SUZANNE RIVECCA'S fiction has been published in *Fence, Story Quarterly, Third Coast,* and other journals. She is a 2005–2007 Wallace Stegner Fellow in fiction at Stanford University in Palo Alto, California. Rivecca has taught literature and creative writing courses at the University of Minnesota, where she received her MFA in creative writing.

LUIS J. RODRIGUEZ'S most recent poetry collection, *My Nature Is Hunger: New and Selected Poems 1989–2004*, won the 2006 Paterson Poetry Prize. He is also the author of a novel, *Music of the Mill*, and of a memoir, *Always Running: La Vida Loca, Gang Days in L.A.* Rodriguez's other books of poetry include *The Concrete River*, which won a PEN West/Josephine Miles Award for Literary Excellence, and *Poems across the Pavement*, which received San Francisco State University's Poetry Center Book Award. He is a regular columnist for the *Progressive* and the founder of Tia Chucha Press, which publishes emerging, socially conscious poets.

RICHARD RODRIGUEZ has worked as a teacher, journalist, and educational consultant, in addition to appearing as a regular essayist on the *NewsHour with Jim Lehrer.* He is the author of *Brown: The Last Discovery of America*, which received the 2003 Melcher Book Award, *Hunger of Memory: The Education of Richard Rodriguez, Mexico's Children*, and *Days of Obliga-*

tion: An Argument with My Mexican Father. In 1997 Rodriguez received the George Foster Peabody Award for his *NewsHour* essays on American life.

DAVID ROMTVEDT is the author of nine books of poetry and prose, including *A Flower Whose Name I Do Not Know*, which was a winner of the 1992 National Poetry Series. His most recent poetry collection is *Some Church*. He is also the author of *Free and Compulsory for All: Stories of Students and Teachers*. Romtvedt spent ten years working with kindergarten through 12th grade students in the artist-in-schools programs of Alaska, Washington, Nevada, and Montana. He is the current Poet Laureate of Wyoming and teaches at the University of Wyoming.

VERN RUTSALA is the author of nine books of poems, including *A Handbook for Writers: New and Selected Prose Poems*, *The Moment's Equation*, a 2005 finalist for the National Book Award, and *How We Spent Our Time*, winner of the 2006 Akron Poetry Prize. Rutsala retired from teaching at Lewis and Clark College in Portland, Oregon, in 2004.

SCOTT RUSSELL SANDERS is the author of more than twenty books, including novels, collections of short fiction, story books for children, and works of personal nonfiction. His essay collections include *Hunting for Hope: A Father's Journeys*, *Making a Home in a Restless World*, and *The Paradise of Bombs*, which won the 1987 Associated Writing Programs Award for Creative Nonfiction. His most recent book is the memoir *A Private History of Awe*. Sanders teaches English and creative writing at Indiana University in Bloomington, Indiana.

SUSAN RICHARDS SHREVE is the author of twelve novels, including *A Student of Living Things* and *Plum and Jaggers*. She has also edited five anthologies and is the author of numerous books for children and young adults, including *Amy Dunn Quits School* and *The Bad Dreams of a Good Girl*. She was the founder of the MFA program in creative writing at George Mason University, where she continues to teach.

THEODORE R. SIZER is the author of numerous books about education, most recently *The Red Pencil: Convictions from Experience in Education*. He is the founder and chairman of the Coalition of Essential Schools, a national network of schools and centers engaged in restructuring and redesigning schools to promote better student learning and achievement. Three of his books, *Horace's Compromise, Horace's School,* and *Horace's Hope*, explore the motivation and the ideas of the Essential School effort. Sizer was a professor and dean at the Harvard Graduate School of Education and the headmaster at Phillips Exeter Academy in Andover. He is University Professor Emeritus at Brown University, where he served as chair of the Education Department.

LARRY SMITH is the author of more than ten books of poetry and fiction, most recently *A River Remains: Poems* and *Faces and Voices: Tales*. He taught for three years at Euclid High School in Euclid, Ohio, and for thirty-three years at Firelands College of Bowling Green State University. Smith is the editor of several anthologies of working-class literature and a critical study of the poet Kenneth Patchen. He is the founder and editor of Bottom Dog Press in Sandusky, Ohio.

GARY SOTO is the author of thirty books for adults, young adults, and children, including *Living up the Street: Narrative Recollections, A Summer Life, Junior College, Buried Onions*, and *The Afterlife*. He serves as Young People's Ambassador for both California Rural Legal Assistance and the United Farm Workers of America. Soto has produced two films for Spanish-speaking children and is an officer in the Royal Chicano Navy based in Fresno, California.

MICHAEL STEINBERG is a memoirist, personal essayist, and founding editor of the literary journal *Fourth Genre: Explorations in Nonfiction*. His memoir, *Still Pitching*, was chosen by *ForeWord Magazine* as the 2003 Independent Press Memoir/Autobiography of the Year. His edited books include *Peninsula: Essays and Memoirs from Michigan, The Fourth Genre: Contemporary Writers of/on Creative Nonfiction*, and *Those Who Do, Can: Teachers Writing, Writers Teaching*. Steinberg has taught writing and creative writing at Michigan State University for twenty-five years and he is currently on the faculty of the Stone Coast/University of Southern Maine low-residency MFA program.

JUDITH GOLD STITZEL taught English and women's studies for thirty-three years at West Virginia University in Morgantown,

West Virginia, where she was the founding director of the Center for Women's Studies. She has published fiction and essays in *College English*, the *Denver Quarterly*, and the Modern Language Association publication, *Stepping off the Pedestal: Academic Women in the South*.

LAWRENCE SUTIN is the author of several books of nonfiction, including *Jack and Rochelle: A Holocaust Story of Love and Resistance*, *A Postcard Memoir*, *All Is Change: The Two-Thousand-Year Journey of Buddhism to the West*, and biographies of Aleister Crowley and Philip K. Dick. He teaches in the MFA program at Hamline University in St. Paul, Minnesota, and the low-residency MFA program at Vermont College.

ANNIE THOMS graduated from Stuyvesant High School in New York City in 1993 and returned to teach English there in 2000. Her book, *With Their Eyes: September 11th—The View from a High School at Ground Zero*, marked the beginning of her work using interview-based monologues with high school students to capture stories and create oral histories of critical issues in school communities. She is coauthor of "The Monologue Project for Creating Vital Drama in Secondary Schools," which was published in *English Journal*.

JANE TOMPKINS is a university professor who taught American literature, literary theory, women's writing, and popular culture for many years before becoming a holistic educator focused on bringing mind, body, emotions, and spirit into the classroom. Her memoir, *A Life in School: What the Teacher Learned*, traces her development from career-oriented scholar to experiential teacher. She has spent the last five years of her life in the academy creating student lounges and cafés and renovating classrooms.

BRUCE WEIGL is the author of thirteen books of poetry, including *The Unraveling Strangeness*, *Declension in the Village of Chung Huang*, and *Archaeology of the Circle: New and Selected Poems*. He is also the author of the best-selling memoir *The Circle of Hanh*. Weigl received the Bronze Star for his service during the Vietnam War and he is coeditor of the multigenre anthology *Between the Lines: Writing on War and Its Social Consequences*. He has published three volumes of poetry in translation from Vietnamese and from Romanian. Weigl is currently Distinguished Professor of Arts and Humanities at Lorain County Community College in Lorain, Ohio.

MEREDITH SUE WILLIS is the author of eleven books of fiction and nonfiction for adults and children. She began working as a writer-in-residence with Teachers and Writers Collaborative in 1971 and was named a distinguished teaching artist for 2000–2003 by the New Jersey State Council on the Arts. Willis also teaches adults at New York University's School of Continuing and Professional Studies. Her novel for children, *Marco's Monster*, based on her residencies in the South Bronx and Brooklyn, was one of *Instructor* magazine's best books for 1997. Her newest novel for children is *Billie of Fish House Lane*.

Acknowledgments

We are grateful to the Department of English, the Research Council, and the Wick Poetry Center of Kent State University for their generous support. The staff of the Kent State University libraries has also been helpful to us in our research. We thank Holly Carver, director of the University of Iowa Press, for her energy and enthusiasm for this anthology, and John and Lynn Sollers and Judith Gold Stitzel, who helped us locate some of the work. We also thank Judith Kirman, who provided indispensable assistance with research, correspondence, and manuscript preparation. We are always grateful for the curiosity and hope of our students and the patience and wisdom of our teachers. A special thanks to our partners, Anna French and Lynn Gregor, for their support and their willingness to make time in their lives for this work.

We are grateful to the authors who have given permission for us to include previously unpublished work in this anthology. We also thank the authors, editors, and publishers who have given their permission to reprint individual pieces.

MARK BRAZAITIS, "The Invisibles." Copyright © 2007 by Mark Brazaitis. Published by permission of the author.

CHRISTOPHER BUCKLEY, "My Time on Earth." Copyright © 2007 by Christopher Buckley. Published by permission of the author.

DAVID CITINO, "Let's Move Our Chairs and Desks Around and See What We Can See." Copyright © 2007 by the Estate of David Citino. Published by permission of Mary Citino.

ROBERT COLES, "Here and Now We Are Walking Together," from *Notre Dame Magazine* (Summer 2003). Copyright © 2003 by Robert Coles. Reprinted by permission of the author.

KATIE DALEY, "The Word according to Mr. Coosak." Copyright © 2007 by Katie Daley. Published by permission of the author.

TOI DERRICOTTE, from *The Black Notebooks: An Interior Journey*, W. W. Norton and Company, Inc. Copyright © 1977 by Toi Derricotte. Published by permission of the author.

ANNIE DILLARD, from *An American Childhood*, Harper and Row Publishers, Inc. Copyright © 1987 by Annie Dillard. Reprinted by permission of the author.

MARK DOTY, from *Firebird: A Memoir*, HarperCollins Publishers. Copyright © 1999 by Mark Doty. Reprinted by permission of the author and HarperCollins Publishers.

VIOLET A. DUTCHER, "Learning Politics in the First Grade." Copyright © 2007 by Violet A. Dutcher. Published by permission of the author.

JOYCE DYER, "The Day I Stopped Hating Cheerleaders." Copyright © 2007 by Joyce Dyer. Published by permission of the author.

LINDA DYER, "Votive," from *Fictional Teeth*, Ahsahta Press. Copyright © 2001 by Linda Dyer. Reprinted by permission of the author.

KATHY EVANS, "After the Facts: Poetry and the Sophomores." Copyright © 2007 by Kathy Evans. Published by permission of the author.

HENRY LOUIS GATES, JR., from *Colored People: A Memoir*, Random House, Inc. Copyright © 1994 by Henry Louis Gates, Jr. Published by permission of the author and Alfred A. Knopf, a division of Random House, Inc.

DIANE GILLIAM, "Does Not Use Free Time Wisely," in *Recipe for Blackberry Cake*, Kent State University Press. Copyright © 1999 by the author. Published by permission of the author.

RICHARD HAGUE, from *Milltown Natural: Essays and Stories from a Life*, Bottom Dog Press. Copyright © 1997 by Richard Hague. Reprinted by permission of the author.

DAVID HASSLER, "Wrestling Mr. Dietz." Copyright © 2007 by David Hassler. Published by permission of the author.

RUTH ELLA HENDRICKS, "Professional Knowledge and Practice." Copyright © 2007 by Ruth Ella Hendricks. Published by permission of the author.

WILLIAM HEYEN, "The End," in *Pig Notes and Dumb Music: Prose on Poetry*, BOA Editions. Copyright © 1998 by William Heyen. Reprinted by permission of the author.

FAITH S. HOLSAERT, "History Dancing." Copyright © 2007 by Faith S. Holsaert. Published by permission of the author.

HANK HUDEPOHL, "Friday Night Heroes." Copyright © 2007 by Hank Hudepohl. Published by permission of the author.

LAWSON FUSAO INADA, "Our Song." Copyright © 2007 by Lawson Fusao Inada. Published by permission of the author.

JULIA SPICHER KASDORF, "Portrait of a Poet as a Public School Kid." Copyright © 2007 by Julia Spicher Kasdorf. Published by permission of the author.

GARRISON KEILLOR, from "School" in *Lake Wobegon Days*, Viking Penguin. Copyright © 1985 by Garrison Keillor. Published by permission of the author and Viking Penguin, a division of Penguin Group (USA) Inc.

JANE KENYON, "Dreams of Math," in *A Hundred White Daffodils*, Graywolf Press. Copyright © 1999 by the Estate of Jane Kenyon. Reprinted by permission of Graywolf Press, Saint Paul, Minnesota.

JESSE LEE KERCHEVAL, from "Everything You Always Wanted to Know," in *Space*, Algonquin Books. Copyright © 1998 by Jesse Lee Kercheval. Reprinted by permission of the author.

BARBARA KINGSOLVER, "How Mr. Dewey Decimal Saved My Life," in *High Tide in Tucson: Essays from Now or Never*, HarperCollins Publishers. Copyright © 1995 by Barbara Kingsolver. Reprinted by permission of HarperCollins Publishers.

LEONARD KRESS, "Yearbook." Copyright © 2007 by Leonard Kress. Published by permission of the author.

STEPHEN KUUSISTO, from *Planet of the Blind*, Dial Press. Copyright © 1998 by Stephen Kuusisto. Reprinted by permission of the author.

PHILIP LEVINE, from *The Bread of Time: Toward an Autobiography*, University of Michigan Press. Copyright © 2001 by Philip Levine. Reprinted by permission of the author.

AUDRE LORDE, from *Zami: A New Spelling of My Name*, Crossing Press. Copyright © 1982 by Audre Lorde. Reprinted by permission of Crossing Press, a division of Ten Speed Press, Berkeley, California. www.tenspeed.com.

PETER MARKUS, "I Am a Cloud: Revisited, or an Open Letter to My Third Grade Teacher." Copyright © 2007 by Peter Markus. Published by permission of the author.

GARY SOTO, "Catholics," in *Living up the Street: Narrative Recollections,* Dell Publishing Company. Copyright © 1985 by Gary Soto. Reprinted by permission of the author.

MICHAEL STEINBERG, "High School Baseball Tryouts" first appeared in part in *Still Pitching: A Memoir,* Michigan State University Press. Copyright © 2003 by Michael Steinberg. Reprinted by permission of the author.

JUDITH GOLD STITZEL, "Milk Money." Copyright © 2007 by Judith Gold Stitzel. Published by permission of the author.

LAWRENCE SUTIN, "One of the Men in the White Coats," in *A Postcard Memoir,* Graywolf Press. Copyright © 2000 by Lawrence Sutin. Reprinted by permission of the author.

ANNIE THOMS, from *With Their Eyes: September 11th—The View from a High School at Ground Zero,* Harper Tempest, an imprint of HarperCollins Publishers. Copyright © 2002 by Annie Thoms. Reprinted by permission of the author.

JANE TOMPKINS, "Reverie," in *A Life in School: What the Teacher Learned,* Perseus Press. Copyright © 1997 by Jane Tompkins. Reprinted by permission of the author.

BRUCE WEIGL, "Before and After," in *The Circle of Hanh: A Memoir,* Grove Press. Copyright © 2000 by Bruce Weigl. Reprinted by permission of the author.

MEREDITH SUE WILLIS, "What I Learned in First Grade." Copyright © 2007 by Meredith Sue Willis. Published by permission of the author.